Ageism:
Prejudice and Discrimination
Against the Elderly

DATED

Lifetime Series in Aging

Available now from Wadsworth:

The Social Forces in Later Life: An Introduction to Social Gerontology, Third Edition
By Robert C. Atchley, Miami University

Social Problems of the Aging: Readings
By Mildred M. Seltzer, Sherry L. Corbett, and Robert C. Atchley, Miami University

The Economics of Aging, Second Edition
By James H. Schulz; Brandeis University

Biology of Aging
By Morris Rockstein and Marvin Sussman, University of Miami; consulting editor, Alan D. Entine, SUNY at Stony Brook

Human Services for Older Adults: Concepts and Skills
By Anita S. Harbert, West Virginia University, and Leon H. Ginsberg, Commissioner, West Virginia Department of Welfare

Families in Later Life
By Lillian E. Troll, Rutgers University, and Sheila J. Miller and Robert C. Atchley, Miami University

Minorities and Aging
By Jacquelyne J. Jackson, Duke University; consulting editor, Alan D. Entine, SUNY at Stony Brook

Gerontology in Higher Education: Perspectives and Issues
Edited by Tom Hickey, Harvey L. Sterns, and Mildred M. Seltzer

Gerontology in Higher Education: Developing Institutional and Community Strength
Edited by Harvey L. Sterns, Edward F. Ansello, Betty Sprouse, and Ruth Layfield-Faux

Available now from Brooks/Cole:

Early and Middle Adulthood: The Best Is Yet to Be—Maybe
By Lillian E. Troll, Rutgers University

Late Adulthood: Perspectives on Human Development
By Richard A. Kalish, Berkeley, California

The Later Years: Social Applications of Gerontology
By Richard A. Kalish, Berkeley, California

Counseling Adults
By Nancy K. Schlossberg, University of Maryland, and Alan D. Entine, SUNY at Stony Brook

Life-Span Developmental Psychology: Introduction to Research Methods
By Paul B. Baltes and John R. Nesselroade, Pennsylvania State University, and Hayne W. Reese, West Virginia University

Available now from Duxbury:

Working with the Elderly: Group Process and Techniques
By Irene Mortenson Burnside

Forthcoming titles from Wadsworth:

Aging: Politics and Policies
By Robert H. Binstock, Brandeis University

Comparative Gerontology: Aging in Various Societies
By Donald O. Cowgill, University of Missouri, Columbia

Ageism:
Prejudice and Discrimination
Against the Elderly

Jack Levin
Northeastern University

William C. Levin
Bridgewater State College

Wadsworth Publishing Company
Belmont, California
A Division of Wadsworth, Inc.

Gerontology Editor: Curt Peoples
Production Editor: Diane Sipes
Copy Editor: Stephen McElroy

Printed in the United States of America

1 2 3 4 5 6 7 8 9 10—84 83 82 81 80

Library of Congress Cataloging in Publication Data

Levin, Jack, 1941 –
    Ageism: prejudice and discrimination against
the elderly

    (Lifetime series in aging)
    Bibliography: p.
    Includes index.
    1. Gerontology—United States.   2. Aged—
United   States.   3. Aging.   4. Age
discrimination—United States.   I. Levin, William
C., joint author.   II. Title.   III. Series.
    HQ1064.U5L48   305.2'6'0973   80–12829
    ISBN 0–534–00881–X

Credits

For Minnie-Mama, Nana, and Oma

Acknowledgments:

Many people have contributed in their professional capacities to this book. We greatly appreciate the work of editors, colleagues, and reviewers—in particular, Charles Longino, University of Miami, Coral Gables; Arnold Arluke, Northeastern University; Beth Hess, County College of Morris; and Robert Bendiksen, University of Wisconsin, La Crosse. We also take this opportunity to express our special thanks to Arnie Arluke, Maggie Kuhn, Evelyn Levin, and Flea Levin, who volunteered ideas and criticisms that helped determine the direction of the book.

Foreword
Maggie Kuhn
Gray Panthers' National Convener

Ageism: Prejudice and Discrimination Against the Elderly is a significant summary of two decades of gerontological research. It is also an important critic of current social theories and policies dealing with the issues of age.

The authors have documented well the ageism that pervades western society and pointed out the impotence of the retirement education and service programs aimed at socializing the victims to their fate. They have also researched the researchers and their biases, detailing the preoccupation with "individual adjustment" (or failure to adjust) to the oppressions of society and the ignorance of the social, economic, and political forces and conditions that segregate, stereotype, and victimize the survivors. The "minority concept" developed in the book points out both the commonalities between racism, sexism, and ageism and the common practice of blaming the victims for their dilemmas. The authors' broad societal-systemic approach is a welcome addition to current gerontological thinking and practice. They clearly believe that basic societal changes are needed, and generally they support the Gray Panther view that the issues of growing up and growing old in America challenge the goals and values of our competitive, wasteful, productivity-centered society.

For example, there is abundant evidence that people's state of health in old age is profoundly related to their social class and affected by poverty and hazardous working and living conditions throughout their lives, rather than only during the so-called "decline" in later years. The disengagement theory of aging, now deemed by gerontologists to have limited usefulness, has widely influenced social policies on aging, particularly in the area of mandatory retirement—generally practiced by corporations, business, industry, and even academic institutions. This policy involves an enormous social waste and a personal trauma from which many workers do not recover. The loss of income, status, and useful role associated with work is societal, not merely personal. The disengagement theory prepared people to step down and out of involvement in community life, increased the dead weight of social apathy, and deprived millions of experienced survivors of the incentive and opportunity to contribute to the world around them. What is needed now is research to demonstrate how skills, experience, and knowledge can be transferred and applied to the complex problems of a new era.

Gerontological theories have also justified such projects as Sun City and Leisure Worlds, as well as federal programs like "section 202" housing, which physically and socially segregate people by chronological age. The ultimate consequences for our society of ghettoization by age have not yet been perceived or assessed.

Gray Panthers are vigorously affirming the need for intergenerational association and action, and, in response to Gray Panther organizing, significant interest is mounting in intergenerational living and the restructuring of the traditional nuclear family in favor of "families of choice," based on mutual interests, goals, and resources, rather than on kinship ties. Urgently needed now are housing alternatives, the development and testing of new models of cooperative housing for young and old people on college campuses, the rehabilitation of existing structures, and changes in lending policies to eliminate "redlining" and urban blight.

So-called "gray power" groups, organized on the basis of the special needs of the elderly, are often contrary to the larger public interest. Indeed, they may increase the alienation of old people from younger members of society. The needs of old people can be important levers for social, economic, and political changes that will benefit all disadvantaged groups. There must be recognition that no group of older Americans will really thrive until societal attitudes and policies change, and until our competitive, wasteful, productivity-centered society becomes truly human and just.

As Simone de Beauvoir observed in *Becoming of Age*, the issues of age put the whole society to the test.

Preface

We are sociologists who have become interested in the problems of aging in America. Before this, much of our time was devoted to studying race and ethnic relations. In part, we focused on stereotyping, prejudice and discrimination, and minority-group status.

As a consequence of our earlier work, we bring to our study of old age in America a perspective different from that of most of the gerontologists who have dominated the field. In fact, it would be surprising if gerontologists did not see us as outsiders who speak with a foreign accent. As Kuhn (1962) suggests, disciplines tend to develop models for studying the world that become entrenched and widely accepted within the discipline. Frequently, such models become so basic to the study of a problem that they take the form of unquestioned assumptions. We believe that this has happened in the field of gerontology.

Specifically, the literature of gerontology has consistently reported and emphasized decline, whether physical, psychological, or social, in the characteristics and capacities of the aged. In Chapter One, we have selected only a few of the findings in each area to illustrate this focus on decline. What may appear to be a rather lengthy review actually represents only a very small sampling of this pervasive tendency.

At first reading, we failed to question the appropriateness of studying characteristics of decline in the aged. The dominant model seemed to make sense. It was not until we re-examined the gerontological literature from another perspective—namely, the perspective employed to study race and ethnic relations—that we saw the stress on characteristics of decline in the aged as extremely limiting and possibly harmful. As we argue in Chapter Two, the literature of gerontology has tended to "blame the victim" by explaining the problems of the aged as consequences of the individual's deterioration and decline. Such a model fails to place adequate emphasis on, and in some cases ignores altogether, the way social forces contribute to the difficulties faced by the aged. This argument is especially applicable to the research findings and theories of social gerontology.

In the search for a model that would *not* blame the elderly for their problems, we also drew on our familiarity with the concepts used in the study of ethnic and race relations. In Chapter Three, we argue that the aged constitute an important minority group, whose members suffer prejudice and discrimination in much the same way as other minority groups. The precedent for the minority perspective has existed at least since Barron's discussion of the aged as a quasi minority in 1953 and certainly since Butler coined the term *ageism* in 1969 to describe discrimination against the elderly. For a number of reasons to be explored in this work, the concept of the aged as a minority group has never been systematically applied, and its validity has been denied by many gerontologists.

In Chapter Four we compare the reactions of the aged to their status in society with the reactions of other minorities to their treatment by society. The appropriateness of applying the minority model to the aged then becomes apparent. As a unifying concept, seeing the aged as a minority group accounts readily for behaviors such as age concealment, alcoholism, senility, and playing the role of senior citizen—apparently disparate elements in the gerontological literature whose relationship to one another was previously ignored or not clear. We believe that policies and programs concerning the aged could be greatly altered, and greatly improved, by a perspective that roots the problems of the aged in social forces rather than individual characteristics.

Chapter Five examines programs that have grown out of the perspective that blames the victim—for example, those aimed at easing the adjustment of the elderly to their assigned status. Based on the minority model, we explore alternative programs directed at modifying those institutions and attitudes that contribute to the diminished status of the elderly.

We must reject or radically modify the prevailing model of the aged as "in decline" and focus on those social forces that are at the foundation of ageism in our society. Continued exclusive attention to the symptoms of aging is a bottomless pit of expense and frustration.

Contents

Chapter One   Gerontology: The Focus on Decline   1
A Focus on the Characteristics of the Aged   2
Physiological Aging   4
Psychological Aging   10
Sociological Aging   19
Maintaining the Age-Related Societal Relationships   31
Summary   33

Chapter Two   Blaming the Aged   35
Blaming the Victim   36
Social Order and Social Problems   39
Blaming the Aged   41
Disengagement Theory   44
Activity Theory   53
Subculture Theory   54
"Helping" the Aged   57
Why We Blame the Aged   60
The Problem of the Young   62
Summary   64

Chapter Three   The Aged as a Minority Group   65
Concept of Minority Group   65
Streib's "Are the Aged a Minority Group?"   66
Sociological Focus of Minority-Group Concept   71
Ageism as a Form of Prejudice and Discrimination   72
Images of the Aged   73
Cultural Aspects of Ageism   85
Theories of Prejudice and Ageism   91
Summary   95

Chapter Four   Reactions to Ageism   97
The Role of Senior Citizen   97
Acceptance   98
Avoidance   102
Aggression   110
Summary   113

Chapter Five   Proposals and Prospects for Change   115

Encouraging Acceptance   115
Encouraging Avoidance   116
Acceptance, Avoidance, and Social Change   117
Influencing System-Change Behavior   118
Retirement as a Form of Age Discrimination   121
Proposals for System Changes   124
Senior Power: the Gray Panthers   124

Bibliography   129

Index   148

Chapter One

Gerontology: The Focus on Decline

This chapter will focus on the historical response of those researchers and scientists who have studied both the process of aging and the social conditions of the aged. The literature of gerontology—the study of all the aspects of aging—is relatively new; most of it has been produced since the turn of the century.

And while the problems associated with aging and the scientific research dealing with it have only recently assumed especial significance in America because the number of elderly in the population has increased and subsequent pressures on the employment and housing markets have also grown, attention to the issues of aging is not new. For centuries human beings have been concerned with the possibilities of prolonging life and, of course, delaying old age and death. Think, for example, of the concern of early scientists and explorers with the search for eternal youth. More recently the beginning of the twentieth century saw the start of *geriatrics* (Freeman, 1960b), the medical study of the physiology and pathology of old age.

By the 1920s the attention of psychologists to the mental adaptive capacities of the aging individual was marked by the publication of G. Stanley Hall's *Senescence* (1923). Just as earlier *physiological* research had focused on the evidences of physical deterioration in the elderly, psychologists now began to study various signs of psychological decline among the aging. Here attention was paid to deterioration of psychological make-up in the areas of perception, mental ability, drives, emotions, motives, and sensory and psychomotor processes.

During the 1940s and 1950s sociologists began to study the aged and the process of aging as social problems. The addition of the sociological perspective to the already existing physiological and psychological perspectives within gerontology was signaled in a statement by

1

Stieglitz. In *Geriatric Medicine: Medical Care of Later Maturity*, he coined the term *social gerontology*, suggesting that "social gerontology concerns man as a social organism, existing in a social environment and being affected by it as well as affecting it" (Stieglitz, 1954: 14). The sociology of aging would focus on the way societal arrangements influence and are influenced by both the process of aging and the well-being of the aged.

The Gerontological Society was organized in 1945, and the first issue of its *Journal of Gerontology* was published the following year. As Streib and Orbach (1967: 616) note, "the first issue carried as its lead article an articulation of the new field. The notable feature of this presentation was its conception of gerontology as a broad multidisciplinary field encompassing both natural and social sciences." Since that time the physiological, psychological, and sociological approaches have dominated research in aging, and anthropology has added a cross-cultural emphasis as well.

Each discipline brought its own methods and history to the developing field, but they were not independent of one another. With its earlier successes in accurate measurement and quantitative procedures, physiological research became a model for psychologists and sociologists. Psychologists assumed that the brain, like the body, must deteriorate with age, so research into the decline of various psychological capacities was pursued. Sociologists assumed that aging individuals must decline socially as well. In fact, more than one social theory of aging held that the inevitability of physical decline brought about social aging as well. The literature in gerontology is shot through both with the assumption of decline with age and, perhaps partly as a result of this assumption, with the findings of physical, psychological, and sociological deterioration in aging individuals.

In order to understand how ageism took root in our society (it is found in laws and government programs developed to deal with the problems of aging), we must discover how researchers in gerontology have approached the study of the aging individual. What questions have they asked about aging , and what assumptions have they brought to their inquiry? How have their findings contributed to a shared view of the process of aging, and how has this led to an ageist perspective?

A Focus on the Characteristics of the Aged

The bulk of this research has focused on characteristics of the aged and on aging as a process rather than on the contexts in which aging proceeds. Examples of this are almost as extensive as the literature itself. In the research on the physiology of aging, every finding of change in the physical capacity of humans with advancing age illustrates the focus on characteristics of aging and the aged. Studies in the psychology of aging also have paid particular attention to characteristics of the aged when focusing on declines in sensory and psychomotor processes, and when examining changes in intellect, personality, and so on. The same tendency to focus on characteristics of the elderly occurs in social gerontology when it examines the extent of their adjustment to role loss or their degree of isolation from the structure of society.

At first, this type of approach may seem to be the most obvious and fruitful way to study aging and the aged; if we wish to understand the problems associated with aging, we must study the aged. However, we should not accept these findings without examining the implications of such an approach. If these finding were merely descriptive, if they were used only to identify and define the characteristics of old people, we might not have to examine the implications of employing such a research approach. However, these finding are not merely descriptive.

Clearly, one needs descriptive data in order to deal with a problem that needs solving. However, it is important to recognize that information is never collected in an intellectual vacuum. The very act of asking a research question implies the existence of a theory about how the world works. For example, think of the assumptions about how the world works that are implied by the research question, "How fast is an object traveling after it has fallen 7 feet?" There are assumptions that some sort of gravitational force exists, that an object might be influenced by it, and that the force will have a measurable and uniform influence on the object. These assumptions are so much a part of our ideas about the operation of the physical world that an investigator may overlook their implications in his or her research. Similarly, the questions that form the basis of research in gerontology imply the existence of a theory about how the world works, whether that world is physical, psychological, or social.

The kinds of questions asked in supposedly descriptive research in gerontology actually reflect an underlying assumption that the characteristics of the aged not only have something to do with the difficulties of aging but that they in fact cause them. The first step in this illogic involves the confusion of association with causation. While we can often identify two or more variables that change together or are associated (such as the tendency of age to increase as psychological capacities decrease), it is quite a different matter to show that changes in one (age) actually *cause* changes in another (psychological capacities). In gerontology so many studies have been conducted that relate age to changes in various human characteristics, that age as the cause of these changes has remained an unchallenged assumption in the field. To conclude the illogic, gerontological literature has seemed to "prove" that since the problems of the aged are shown to be related to changes in the characteristics of the aged, then it must be those characteristics which the aged inevitably develop that *cause* the problems!

A review of the gerontological literature clearly shows that physiologists, psychologists, and sociologists of aging have all shared this important assumption about aging. This view is so persistent, not only among gerontologists but also in the rest of society, that we have come to view its various findings as the truth about an inevitable process of individual decline.

But the accuracy of gerontological research is only part of the problem. Our main concern in this book is the way in which shared assumptions about aging have limited the type of questions that gerontologists have been able or willing to ask.

Physiological Aging

Biologists, physicians, and chemists who study aging and the aged all share an interest in the manifestations of physiological aging, and in how its undesirable effects may be controlled. As we age, changes in our appearance become apparent. During the early years of life these changes are associated with the process we call growth or maturation. When these changes occur as we grow older, they are considered the process of aging. And as noted by Breen (1960: 150) "physiologists and biologists virtually universally look upon aging as a period of decline." The term used to refer to this physiological deterioration is *senescence,* defined by Comfort (1964b: 22) as "a decrease in viability and an increase in vulnerability . . . an increasing probability of death with increasing chronological age." In this sense then, senescence is seen as applying to anyone who lives long enough to develop wrinkled skin or reduced muscle tone, or who develops any of the many diseases more likely to strike an old rather than a young person.

Some Cosmetic Signs of Physiological Aging

Senescence is a term that physiologists of aging have developed to describe the losses in physical capacity common among the aged and is the result of a series of interdependent processes that occur at widely varying rates among individuals (Strehler, 1962). The signs of this process are readily visible in cosmetic changes, such as changes in hair color, in skin tone and texture, but are also present in the less visible operations of the organism, such as cell reproduction. Because individuals age at different rates, studying senescence or physical aging is often difficult. For example, hair may begin to gray or thin out while a person is still in the mid-twenties, or it may never happen at all, and serious diseases that plague the aged may also strike younger individuals. Thus, generalizations by researchers about the signs of aging must be the result of the average measure on some sign of aging (for example, muscle tone) for a group of people who have lived for the same number of years. A truly accurate description of the effects of aging on the body would have to identify not only all the symptoms of such aging, but the influence that each symptom has on the others—for example, might a person concerned about his graying hair, stop exercising, and so lose muscle tone? Satisfactory conclusions are not easily reached.

Some researchers such as Comfort (1964a), and Heron and Chown (1967) have even suggested that chronological age is useless as an indicator of physiological decline among humans. But however inaccurate we may be in judging the age of a person who *looks* old, we still commonly make such evaluations on the basis of physical characteristics. In a similar way, physicians commonly associate certain diseases with old age, or age-graded health in a patient, suggesting that "you have the heart of a person half your age," or warning that "your blood pressure is that of an older man's." The apparently strong association between physical decline and advancing age helps explain the practice of chronological diagnosis in which a person's age is used as a clue to the illnesses he or she is to be suspected of suffering.

Old age, then, is at least partly in the eye of the beholder, and those cosmetic changes that we associate with old age may be more socially than biologically real. They are, nonetheless, one way we judge old age. Primary among them is the appearance of the skin. It tends to become wrinkled and, in some places, flaccid, and it develops areas of dark pigment (which one current television commercial calls age spots). The skin becomes increasingly sensitive to bruises and discolorations, and heals more slowly. Also reported as associated with old age is the tendency of hair to turn gray or silvery (actually the loss of pigment) or, primarily among males, to fall out.

Research has reported that loss of muscle strength and changes in the structure of the spine may give rise to the bent posture associated with old age. The stiffening of joints contributes to this posture, slowing the speed of movement generally, and accentuating the loss in reaction time. Hearing and sight loss also contribute to the apparent differences between the old and the rest of the population.

When seen in combination, such physical characteristics are striking to even the most casual observer. In fact, we have so come to expect an old person to look and act like this, that the absence of any of these characteristics in an older person often elicits disbelief or condescension: ''She certainly has nice skin—for a person that old.''

By themselves these cosmetic characteristics would probably not be of major concern to either the elderly or the rest of society. However, they are taken to be indicators of further physiological aging that is not so obvious to the observer or to the aging person. As with the cosmetic changes associated with aging, these internal changes vary widely among individuals, but unlike the cosmetic signs of aging, these are much more directly associated with the illnesses that are primary killers of the old.

Physiological Aging and Disease

The association between the onset of old age and the increased incidence of serious illness is striking. According to a report of the U.S. Department of Health, Education, and Welfare (1971) that compared health statistics for persons between the ages of 45 and 64 with those for persons over 65, the elderly suffer greater rates of each of the following illnesses: heart disease, hypertension, arthritis, diabetes, nervous breakdown, dental problems, visual problems, hearing problems, mental and nervous conditions, ulcer, cancer, and more. One striking illustration of the increased incidence of serious illness in the elderly is apparent in the reports that an American male over 65 years old is 5 times more likely to die of heart disease than a person between the ages of 45 and 64, and 10 times more likely to die of cerebrovascular disease.

Heart disease is the greatest cause of death among the aged (United States Department of Health, Education, and Welfare, 1971). While there is no single cause for these deaths, changes in the cardiovascular system associated with aging are shown to be involved. Reduced elasticity of valve and vessel tissues, the build-up of fatty and calcium salt deposits, and the weakening of the heart muscle itself are among the factors that contribute to the likelihood of heart failure.

Cerebrovascular diseases such as stroke and senile dementia (senility) are great cripplers and killers of the aged. According to medical research failures in the circulatory system of an older person reduce the flow of blood, and therefore of oxygen, to the brain leading to these illnesses. In addition, the brain appears to suffer both fluid and cell loss in older age, and a reduction in the speed of neural impulses in the central nervous system slows reaction time in the aged.

While degeneration of the circulatory and nervous systems has been directly linked to catastrophic diseases in the elderly, the degeneration of other bodily systems, though not necessarily linked to illnesses as deadly to the old as stroke or heart disease, does contribute to the often cumulatively ill health that makes operation in the everyday world impossible for some old people. Changes in the efficiency and capacity of the reproductive, digestive, respiratory, and temperature control systems of the human body may lead to serious illnesses for some. For example, changes in the female reproductive system that accompany old age, such as menopause, may result in very difficult episodes of irritability and energy loss. And the emphysema or bronchitis resulting from degeneration of the respiratory system have been shown to be quite serious consequences.

Geriatric Medicine. While the effect of any one of these system declines may be slight, it is still likely to interact with the effects of others, and the overall negative influence on the ability of the older person to operate will be cumulative. And because physiological aging is reported to result from the deterioration of many systems of the body, the practice of geriatric medicine is difficult. It is possible that no single factor is causing a patient's suffering, and sometimes the treatment of one source of the complaint may actually worsen some other facet of it.

Faced with such complex sets of illnesses among such a large group of people, geriatric medicine has had to be content with what is essentially a holding action. "In an age of improved medical knowledge and skills (insulin, liver extract, vitamins, antibiotics, steroids, radiation therapy, new forms of surgical intervention) there are therapeutic measures by which a number of acute and some chronic conditions may be delayed or stopped. Even if a cure is not obtainable, there are means of deferring or altering the threat of acute conditions. When a complete cure is not possible, some forms of chronicity with independent survival may be attained" (Freeman, 1960a: 25). Nonetheless, the diseases of the elderly and their causes have become the subject of a great deal of medical research.

Theories of Physiological Aging

It is one thing to note the relationship between chronological aging and the illnesses that the deterioration of various human systems cause. It is quite another to discover why such deterioration occurs. Without the discovery of the root cause or causes, we are doomed to fight the diseases of the aged in a holding action, constantly struggling with the symptoms of physical aging, and measuring success by the small amounts of time gained. Research into and theorizing about the causes of aging have long been a part of the gerontological literature.

And beyond simply describing the varying rates of senescence within any species of animal, investigators have proposed a number of theories as to the physiological causes of aging. These inquiries assume that even if humans did not die of catastrophic illness or accidents the loss of their energies and ability to resist disease would eventually cause their death. Some early theories of aging held that old age is itself a disease (Bogomolets, 1946; Korenchevsky, 1950) or at least that old age has some diseases of its own (Howell, 1949a). According to such notions, one catches old age as one catches any illness, and if it were not contracted as a disease, one might live on indefinitely. While this position is not currently popular among researchers into the physiology of aging, it is an example of one approach the field has taken.

More recently, books such as Bernard Strehler's *Time, Cells, and Aging* (1962), Alex Comfort's *The Biology of Senescence* (1964), and Robert Kohn's *Principles of Mammalian Aging* (1971), contain ideas about aging that range from the purely common-sense notions that human organisms simply wear out to the more complex possibilities of biochemical theories of aging.

Among these theories are the following.

A person may be expected to live approximately as long as his or her heritage will allow. That is to say that one inherits from one's parents a relatively fixed life span just as one may inherit eye color or height (Freeman, 1960a). This type of "biological clock" notion is supported by evidence of families that have long-living members.

A second theory suggests that mechanical wear and tear may, over years of operation, cause the aging of substructures of the human organism, and cumulatively of the overall organism. As the parts of any machine wear down, the machine itself must one day stop operating, and the analogy with the human body seems apt. This idea is used in Kohn's discussion of chemical aging—"structures of macromolecules subjected to repeated and prolonged stresses may be damaged. Membranes and fibers may become fragmented or split, or may develop perforations" (1971: 17).

Kohn (1971) also discusses the contribution to aging made by the accumulation in cells of various products of the operation of the human organism. In some processes this accumulation is functional for the organism, as in the production and accumulation of keratin when the skin tans. It is therefore not always appropriate to call these accumulations waste products. But when the rate of synthesis of these products becomes greater than the cells' ability to dispose of them, the process may become dysfunctional, and the body's equilibrium will be disrupted. In this regard physiological research has investigated the effect of accumulation of minerals in the cells as a mechanism of physical aging.

The previous theory, which focused on processes inside the cells, has a parallel theory focusing on processes outside the cells, primarily on connective tissue. This theory proposes that collagen, the primary component in human connective tissue, swells and stiffens with age with consequences for the efficiency of operation of the human organism. Since human skin, bone, tendon, and ligaments are composed of a high percentage of extracellular material, they are quite likely to be affected by the deterioration of collagen, and it is in these areas that the cosmetic changes and reductions in mobility among the aged may be critical.

The observed reduction in the efficiency of the body's immune system as we age accounts for a further theory. The immune system helps us fight off disease, but as we age it weakens, and what we were previously able to ward off, now takes hold. According to this theory, old-age diseases are really diseases of any age, which, due to weakened immune systems, are simply more likely to take hold in the elderly.

One of the most promising of the new theories of aging deals with the way cells reproduce themselves. For a variety of reasons, cells sometimes fail to reproduce themselves accurately. As the number of these mutations increases in the body, a variety of effects are thought to occur relative to the aging of the organism. Three such effects:

> "1. . . . The mutant cells are not recognized by cells of the immune system, so they attack the 'intruder' (this is called an autoimmune response);
> 2. . . . multiplication of mutant cells itself results in displacement of normal cells and consequent malfunction;
> 3. . . . mutant cells produce so many 'errors' in the response of cells to given conditions that the organism sickens and dies."
> (Cottrell, 1974: 8)

Whatever causes aging, and any or all of the preceding theories may prove true, it is clear that the onset of physiological aging and the rate at which it occurs are highly variable among individuals, and that scientific research has focused on the physiological symptoms and causes of aging.

Both the theories and the research in physiological aging have contributed to our expectation that the human organism will deteriorate with age. This work has become increasingly detailed and quantitative. While we may cling to the hope that some previously secret key to longer (or even permanent) life may be found hidden in the chemistry of life, we accept in the meantime our inevitable physical decline and death. We see this process as natural and of the order of things beyond our control. We accept our fate to be sure, but we must not assume that physiological decline means inevitable decline in other areas of our lives, such as in our mental capacities. Psychologists of aging seem to have taken the literature of physiological aging as a model for their own work, assuming that the brain declines with age as the rest of the body does. Thus, like the literature in physiological aging, the psychology of aging has become a litany of decline in the mental adaptive capacities of humans.

Psychological Aging

Lower animals depend for their survival on inborn or instinctual responses to the demands of the environment. Humans, however, respond to the environment at least in part by learning from other people appropriate responses to the stimuli surrounding them. Psychology is concerned with those mental processes of individuals which allow them to adapt to their environment. Just as specialists in psychology have studied developmental psychology (how these capacities develop) and abnormal psychology (disruptions or deviations in adaptive capacities), so psychologists of aging have come to be interested in "the age-related adaptive capacities of the individual" (Birren, 1959: 18).

Just as physiological research into aging has demonstrated the deterioration of physical abilities with age, so psychological research has focused on the loss of our mental adaptive capacities. In order to see how the psychology of aging has done this, we shall divide the psychological processes into some component parts using a variation of James Birren's organizational scheme in his authoritative *Handbook of Aging and the Individual* (1959).

Sensory and Perceptual Processes

In order to be able to interact with the environment, we need to gather information about it. The sensory organs such as eyes and ears experience the environment, then send messages about that experience to the brain. The environment experienced (whether external or internal) is different for everyone partly due to the differences in our sensory processes. For example, some people see colors more vividly than others or are more sensitive to changes in temperature or volume. Similarly, if a person's *sensory threshold* is high (this is the level of stimulation necessary before sensory information is sent to the brain), then such a person might not be aware at all of a particular stimulus in the environment.

Research on the changes in sensory threshold and sensory perception that accompany aging has emphasized losses in vision among the elderly (Weale, 1963). According to a 1971 study of the United States Department of Health, Education, and Welfare, "moderate to severely defective visual acuity is about twice as prevalent among older persons as among the middle aged" (HEW, 1971: 25). Bromley (1974: 103) suggests that "degenerative changes in the eye accumulate with age, and diseases increase in frequency." Among the myriad studies that have supported such conclusions are the following, each of which contributes to the finding of vision loss in older age: color discrimination (Lakowski, 1961); light sensitivity (Burg, 1967); depth perception (Bell, Wolf, and Bernholz, 1972); speed of pupil contraction (Kumnick, 1956); speed of adaption to dark (Botwinick, 1973); pupil size and reaction efficiency (Howell, 1949b), and incidence of cataracts (Kornzweig, Feldstein, and Schneider, 1957).

Sight is pehaps the single most important sense we use in daily operation in the world. It is extremely important to our mobility. Hearing is probably second in importance to sight (think of the consequences if you could not use the telephone or hear normal conversation) and has also been studied at length. As with vision, hearing has been reported to decline with age (for example, Beasley, 1940; Bergman, 1971). The study of hearing loss is unlike the study of vision loss in that the structural changes accompanying hearing loss are not apparent. However, hearing is reported to gradually decrease with the years and is measurable in such vital characteristics as *intensity threshold*, the level of sound intensity necessary to produce hearing. For example, Botwinick (1973) found intensity threshold to be greater among older people than among younger people, and Konig (1957) found deterioration in frequency discrimination with age. The other senses—taste, smell, balance, and touch—also have been found to decline generally in efficiency with age (for example, Hinchcliffe, 1962; Schiffman, 1977; Schiffman and Pasternak, 1979).

Perceptual processes, whereby meaning is attached to stimuli, are intimately linked with sensory processes. Sometimes the stimuli and their meaning are relatively simple (Verplanck, 1957). Here the concern is with such sense perceptions as sight, hearing, and so on, as discussed above. However, stimuli and responses may also involve *abstract* rather than simple meaning. For example, it is much less abstract a process to be sensitive to changes in light or sound than to be sensitive to the passage of time, or the relationship between elements of an object and the entire object. Older people have been found to underestimate the passage of time (Feifel, 1957), and according to Braun (1959: 559), "older individuals are, in general, less able to discriminate or recognize ambiguous stimuli and concealed and masked figures."

Psychomotor Performance

Psychomotor performance involves a chain of events leading from experience of a stimulus to the reaction of the organism (if one is called for) to that stimulus. One must first gather information about the stimulus (sensory experience), then evaluate that information (perception). Once the information is integrated with other information in the brain a decision as to any action is made. The message to the appropriate implementing organ (effector) is then sent and the effector is activated. Reductions in the speed, capacity, or accuracy of any item in this complex chain of events would affect any measurement of psychomotor performance. The already illustrated reductions in sensory and perceptual processes among the aged would clearly reduce the efficiency of their psychomotor performance as well. Welford (1959, 1977) has studied psychomotor performance and has noted "relatively little change of speed or accuracy among older people with very simple tasks such as classical reaction-time measures. Changes are greater when movements have to be carried out in a continuous coordinated series" (Welford, 1959: 610).

This relationship between age and declining psychomotor performance of complex tasks has prompted studies into the effects of age on the ability to perform certain types of jobs (McFarland and O'Doherty, 1959) and the effects of age on work-related accidents (King and Speakman, 1953). (This issue is important in our mechanized work world with its emphasis on adaptation of the worker to a machine's pace.)

In general, the findings in the studies of psychomotor performance among the aged support the idea that with age comes what Birren (1968a) has called psychomotor slowness. In a review of the psychological aspects of aging, Birren notes also that " . . . slowness defined as a minimum operations time in the nervous system can be

used in turn to explain other psychological phenomena of aging . . . ''
(1968: 180). This further illustrates the interdependence of systems in
the normal operation of the human organism, and the likelihood that
aging in one system will effect the efficiency of others.

Learning

The interdependence of human systems in the aging process is
particularly important for the study of learning ability. Learning, which
refers to the ability to acquire knowledge or skills through some sort of
experience, has consistently been reported to decline with age
(Jerome, 1959; Atchley, 1977). However, the reported tendency of
learning performance to decline with age is often attributed to decline
in other processes, especially in perception, motivation, physiological
condition, and psychomotor performance (Jerome, 1959; Birren,
1968a). Psychologists studying the age-related changes in learning have
tended to study lower animals so as to reduce some of the difficult
intervening variables like motivation that occur with human subjects
(Hovland, 1951).

Intelligence

Intelligence is as abstract a concept as learning. Like learning,
intelligence is not directly observable and must be inferred from the
responses people make to tests devised to measure such things as
ability to deal with abstraction, to remember, to learn, and to adapt to
and deal with new situations. Research into intelligence is quite complex.

While many studies have shown the tendency for intelligence
scores to decrease with age (Foster and Taylor, 1920; Beeson, 1920;
Willoughby, 1927; Miles, 1934; Wechsler, 1944; Botwinick, 1973), psychologists have also emphasized some of the factors that might have
contributed to such results. For example, Kuhlen (1968a) has claimed
that changes in the culture may invalidate the results of cross-sectional
studies of the relationship between age and intelligence because intelligence tests have not been shown to be independent of the culture in
which they are composed. Therefore, an older person taking an intelligence test that reflects cultural elements that did not exist during his or
her years of education would be at a disadvantage to a younger person
taking the same test. Baltes and Schaie (1974) suggest that cross-
sectional studies of I.Q. scores—those comparing different age groups
at the same time—continue to show age-related I.Q. differences. But

when measured longitudinally—over a life span—most elements of I.Q. remain stable or even increase. Koller (1968) notes that intelligence test scores may also be influenced by such factors as speed, motivation, and sensory and perceptual processes. Furry and Baltes (1973) suggest that fatigue while taking I.Q. tests may create differences in scores that are usually attributed to age. Atchley (1977) points out that the calculation of normal intelligence for the purpose of age-comparisons has an age-bias built in, placing older individuals at a statistical disadvantage to younger persons.

Memory

With the exception of psychomotor speed, memory is probably that process that is most commonly thought to deteriorate seriously with age. A common stereotype describes old people as incapable of remembering recent events, but able to describe in detail what happened 40 years before. Studies by psychologists have noted the difference between short (a few seconds or minutes), recent (from an hour to a few days), and remote (many years before) types of memory. As with other mental processes, a poor memory at any of these levels is likely to influence other processes such as intelligence and learning, and, in turn, to be influenced by them (Jones, 1959). Studies of the effect of aging on memory seem to show loss of memory ability, of all types, with age (for example, Botwinick, 1967; Craik, 1977).

Creativity, Problem Solving and Thinking

Creativity, problem solving, and thinking are all facets of the ability to manipulate information about the environment, both internal and external. We select, order, reorder, compare, contrast, and synthesize from this available information and so create new information. The term *thinking* focuses on the categorization of information in terms of the shared characteristics of varied experiences. *Problem solving* deals with making logical decisions about the uses of categorized information. *Creativity* is the expressive or imaginative manipulation of information to forge something new—such as a book, a painting, an idea. Little is known about the way these processes actually work. Since each of these skills depends upon other processes such as learning, memory, and perception, any findings of decline in the ability to synthesize information may not be clearly attributed to decline in the synthesis skills alone.

Creativity and Aging.   In his classic studies of creativity and aging, Lehman (1953) compiled information about the age at which various individuals made contributions to art, music, technology, literature, medicine, science, entertainment, industry, sports, and so on. Although he found the years of greatest creative productivity to vary between fields, a general finding was that both the amount and the level of creative production tended to decline with advancing age.

Beyond the obvious difficulty of judging the quality of creative work, psychologists have noted other difficulties in establishing a relationship between advancing age and declining creativity. Bromley (1974: 218–219) mentions "a decline in imagination; a decline in the speed of mental processes; a reduction in the amount of time devoted to creative work; loss of contact with creative people and new ideas; changes in interpersonal rivalry and cooperation; changes in the nature of scientific achievement, say from personal research to supervision of others; diminished incentives—pay, conditions, prestige and promotion—for creative work; failure to keep up with changes in scientific activity, as in the greater use of mathematics, computers and electronic instruments, and with new research methods and concepts; a disinclination to take professional risks"—all of which may have a greater effect on creativity than aging.

In addition, there is Lehman's (1953) own list of possible contributory causes for the decline of creative production with age—losses in physical strength, deterioration in sensory and psychomotor skills, physical health, and motivation. (This list of contributing causes probably results from the fact that Lehman was measuring achievement rather than creativity.) Finally, at this level of complexity, human skills are dependent upon a structure of supporting skills and processes so interdependent and complex that decline in any one of them is likely to have consequences for systems throughout the structure.

Drives and Motives

The needs for food, sex, and activity have been recognized by psychologists to be primary drives in human behavior. Drives vary greatly between individuals, and the possibility that drives also vary with age has been investigated by psychologists of aging.

Sex and Aging.   The well-known study of human sexual behavior by Masters and Johnson (1966) has supported the generally held belief that sexual activity (and by inference, sexual drive) declines with age, especially in the male, but this study and others have also emphasized that sexual activity does not decline with age nearly to the extent commonly believed (Lobsenz, 1974; Felstein, 1973; Botwinick, 1973). In addition, apparent reduction in the sex drive cannot be clearly attributed to biological as opposed to psychological or other causes. For example, Masters and Johnson (1966) suggest that in the female reduced sexual activity with age is due largely to hormone changes that make sexual intercourse painful. However, they also recognize that reduced opportunity for sex may contribute to reduction in sexual activity. Similarly, physical or psychological decline such as has already been discussed may make sex not only more difficult but also less appealing—especially among those who maintain an image of sex as an activity primarily for the young (Cottrell, 1974; Rubin, 1965). Other factors that may contribute to this decline include boredom or overfamiliarity with one's partner, reduced compatibility with one's partner, preoccupation with one's career, or fear of failure (Atchley, 1977).

Appetite, Activity, and Aging. Investigations of hunger and activity have primarily been conducted with animals, and while these studies do suggest some reduction in both general levels of hunger and spontaneous activity with age (Botwinick, 1959; Schiffman and Pasternak, 1979), their application to human drive level is not clear. For example, among humans the desire to eat may be influenced very heavily by the surroundings in which food is placed or even the availability of pleasant company with whom a meal may be shared (Cottrell, 1974). Similarly, human activity may be reduced severely by the belief that nothing is worth doing. In either of these instances of human behavior the inference of lowered drive level probably should not be made. No such problems in interpretation are raised in experiments with animals.

Influence of Motivation on Hunger and Activity. Motivation is the mediation of drives by learned preferences. As an example, think of the person who is hungry, but has only unappealing food for a meal, and must eat alone. While all humans may have hunger drives, we learn ways of directing the drive to eat. In American culture we tend to treat eating as a social event, one meant to be pleasant. The pleasure is derived from both the taste of the food and the company in which it is eaten. Deprived of both sources of pleasure it would not be surprising to find a person eating less, and with less pleasure. Similarly, the drive toward activity is motivated in our culture by a number of factors, such as wealth, promotion or progress, status, and so on. Denied these rewards, activity would be stripped of much of its value to us, and so we might exhibit less activity.

Large-Scale Motivational Patterns. These examples of motivation are rather small scale, intended to illustrate the influence of motivation on drives such as hunger and activity. However, large-scale motivational patterns in human behavior have been hypothesized and their relationship to aging suggested. Kuhlen (1968b), for example, suggests that youth is dominated by what he calls "growth and expansion" motivational patterns. He hypothesizes that as we age the satisfaction derived from growth-expansion motives becomes more vicarious, focusing more and more on our children. Eventually growth-expansion motivation disappears and in the elderly is replaced by anxiety and susceptibility to threat as the primary motivator of human behavior.

Accordingly, "the evidence seems particularly clear that anxiety and susceptibility to threat increase with the passage of time and that this circumstance tends to be the motivational source for many of the behavioral (personality) changes that occur with age" such as conservatism, intolerance of ambiguity, and rigidity (Kuhlen, 1968b: 136).

Personality

To this point the discussion of the psychological elements of aging has followed a general pattern of increasing interdependence and complexity of human systems. Beginning with sensory experience and proceeding through intelligence and the way drives are channeled (motivation), each element of human psychological make-up has been related to the others. Their influence on aging has appeared to be interdependent.

We now arrive at the most abstract and complex level of the psychology of aging, the level of the personality. *Personality* refers to the relatively enduring and unique combination of all those mental traits that makes individuals distinct from one another and enables them to orient themselves to their environment and to one another. These traits include learning, motivation, sensation, perception, memory, and so on. Theories of personality have varied widely in terms of the components of personality they have stressed and in the sources of the personality they have identified. One debate has been between those theorists who see personality as being formed during childhood and then remaining relatively stable during the rest of the adult life, and those who see personality as the product of continuing interaction with the environment, capable of change as changes in the environment occur (Inkeles and Levinson, 1969).

Psychologists who have studied the relationship between personality and aging have viewed the issue from at least two perspectives. From a developmental perspective, personality is seen as changing during the life cycle. In the second view the role of personality in adaptation to aging has been investigated. (In the first view, a perception of personality as capable of change is necessary whereas in the second it is not.)

In discussing the role of personality in aging, Breen (1960: 153) notes the accumulation of studies on both "the personality of older persons and on personality changes with age. Earlier writings about the personality of older persons spoke of their 'conservatism,' 'resistance to change,' or 'rigidity.' " These still commonly held beliefs about the elderly imply that personality changes as one grows older, and that conservatism, for example, is characteristic of old age in the culture at large.

Neugarten and her associates (1964) described the development of personality in older age in three areas:

1. The covert or internal area of personality—the way persons see themselves in relation to the environment—becomes increasingly important to the individual;
2. The adaptive, goal-directed components of personality—those concerned with coming to terms with the life situation—are found to display no change with age;
3. The social-interactional components of personality—those concerned with role performance, interaction and involvement—are found to decrease with age.

These descriptions of personality development in the later years have been applied to the study of the adaptation of the elderly to aging. For example, the characteristics of a number of personality types among the aged, described by Reichard, Livson, and Petersen (1962) were found to be important in making a successful adjustment to aging. The authors determined that those who were typically constructive in their view of life rather than negative or impulsive, who were dependent and easy-going, or who were actively engaged in the effort to avoid dependence adjusted well to aging. Those who were either hostile toward the world and angry with others when things went wrong, or who were self-haters who blamed themselves for their own difficulties were found to have adjusted poorly to aging.

The relationship of the personality to adjustments to aging was further elaborated when related to levels of activity and to life satisfaction (Havighurst, Neugarten, and Tobin, 1964; Havighurst, 1968a). In these studies it was shown that life-satisfaction could be high whether one was active in old age or inactive, the determining factor being personality type. For example, older individuals with "integrated" personalities may exhibit low activity levels but have high life-satisfaction if they are "disengaged" types. For "reorganizers" high levels of activity are associated with high life satisfaction.

The literature of the psychology of aging has been dominated by findings of decline in our individual capacities. Decreasing vision, hearing, psychomotor speed and accuracy, learning ability, memory, intelligence, creativity, flexibility, and how one relates to one's surroundings—all of these and others—are areas of human mental adaptive capacities that have been reported to deteriorate with age. Research indicates that individual mental, adaptive capacities that do not decrease, or that actually increase with age, are few.

Sociological Aging

As in the physiology of aging, the psychology of aging has presented a list of characteristics in which deterioration is consistently found. The effect is to make decline with age seem as inevitable for our psychological lives as it is for our bodies. An examination of the literature of social gerontology reveals that like the physiologists and psychologists, social researchers have focused on decline in individuals as they age. The difference is that here the individual is found to decline in his or her social connection with the environment. Typically, such deterioration in the bond between the individual and society is attributed to the losses in physiological and psychological characteristics that we have just presented. In this way, the three fields are interconnected so as to make individual decline seem not only inevitable, but cumulative.

The study of the physiological and psychological aspects of aging dealt with aging as a phenomenon of the individual organism and of the psychological being. Humans, however, are social beings as well, whose condition not only influences, but is influenced by social or group circumstances. In fact, due to the particular way in which we relate to one another, it may be that our well-being is much more dependent upon our social condition than is that of any other animal. For this reason it is especially important to examine how sociologists have studied aging.

Socialization

Briefly, let's examine human social order before moving into the area of sociological aging. Through our interaction with one another we develop ideas about what we think is appropriate behavior, what is worth doing, and how our efforts should be organized in the pursuit of our goals. These ideas and values, and the actions they control, differ in different cultures. But whatever shape a culture takes, it is the result of its *human* members' definitions and perceptions of the world.

 Through socialization, members of a culture are taught how they are expected to behave, and how they are to fulfill the functions or positions available to them. These arrangements cannot be separated from the physical and ideational environment in which they occur, and so they may change with changes in those environments. Thus, the sudden availability of easily collected food in a culture in which food had been scarce would have a number of effects. Food itself might come to be valued differently, and the act of getting it might be viewed with less reverence. Those who had skill at getting food would likely have held high status in the culture, but with the new abundance of food their status would be comparatively lower. Perhaps a new group of people would experience a rise in status, for example those with skill in accounting for newly stored food surpluses or those with skill in trading surplus food for other goods.

Sociologists study the complex relationships between groups of people that develop and shift in human social orders. They examine the human structures created in the family, in urban areas, between poor and wealthy people, between various racial and religious groups in a culture, in medical and other occupational groups, and between the aged and the rest of society.

Social gerontologists have studied the ways in which various age groups are related to the society in which they live, and particularly the relationships between the aged and the rest of society. In the latter case, they have focused on descriptions of these relationships and their consequences—such as isolation, economic dependence, role loss—and on the relationship between the elderly and such social structures as the family, the community, and the economy. They have studied how these relationships are maintained (for example socialization, the way culture is transmitted from one generation to another), and how norms for the behavior of the aged have been developed and maintained. The remainder of this chapter will focus on how social gerontology has described both the relationship between the elderly and our social structures and the mechanisms for the maintenance of those relationships over time.

Some Social Structures and the Aged

What is the place of the elderly in American society? Although the age at which one is considered old varies from culture to culture, all societies seem to have an old population. However, the elderly are not all treated the same, nor are they valued in the same way, in different societies. Social gerontologists have studied the relationship of the aged to the rest of society and found that in modern industrialized societies like the United States, aging is generally accompanied by decreasing social connection with the rest of society, and in some cases, by actual isolation.

Role Loss and Role Change.   As members of society we act according to the expectations others have of us. In any particular social position or status, such as teacher, friend, or parent, the appropriate norms or expectations of behavior spell out a role. For example, the role of teacher includes assigning papers, giving lectures and tests, and taking attendance. The role of parent includes paying for the support of children, giving advice and comfort, and setting rules for children's behavior. At any one time an individual is likely to occupy a number of roles, and throughout his or her life these roles are likely to change. The role of child gives way to the role of parent, student, worker, or perhaps all three. Typically as one grows, a lost set of roles is replaced by a new set. In this developmental view, old age is unique in that lost roles are not replaced, and old age, as in the physiological and psychological perspectives, is characterized by a form of decline, this one sociological.

A number of studies have shown the tendency for social roles to decrease in either number or intensity as we age (Bellin, 1961; Blau, 1961; Phillips, 1957, 1961; Cumming and Henry, 1961). Cumming and Henry (1961) in measuring role loss used a very broad indicator that included interaction with others as a family member, relative, friend, neighbor, worker, churchgoer, shopper, and so on. They counted the number of contacts a person made in any of these roles and concluded that older males tended to lose the formal roles associated with occupation whereas females tended to lose those roles associated with life as a homemaker.

A5792

Similar findings about the type and degree of social interactions by the aged have been reported by Neugarten (1977: 72), who notes, "Here our studies have shown long-term decrease with age on several different measures: on social role performance in various life roles, on the amount of each day a person spends in interaction with others, and in the degree of ego investment in present social roles."

Beyond studying the outright loss of roles among the aged sociologists have described some of the role changes that seem to accompany aging. Phillips (1957: 212) notes that such changes may include

"1. retirement from full-time employment by men and relinquishment of household management by women,
 2. withdrawal from active community and organizational leadership,
 3. breaking up of marriage through the death of one's mate,
 4. loss of an independent household,
 5. loss of interest in distant goals and plans,
 6. acceptance of dependence upon others for support or advice and management of funds,
 7. acceptance of subordinate position to adult offspring or to social workers,
 8. taking up of membership in groups made up largely of old people, and
 9. acceptance of planning in terms of immediate goals."

The types of role changes mentioned here include changes in the family life (from married person to widow or widower), in the occupational life (from working person to retired person), and in the economic life (from earning person to nonearner). In sum, these role changes combine to create the general role of dependent person. The dependent person may need help in planning for housing and transportation, money from others, and so on. To the extent that such dependency increases with age, the role of dependent becomes synonymous with the role of old person, and as a result, we come to *expect* an old person to behave as a dependent. We are often at a loss when an old person does not conform to our idea of "old person." The expectations of behavior held by younger populations about the aged and the expectations of the elderly about themselves have been thoroughly studied (McTavish, 1971), and these findings will be discussed later in a section on how age-related structures are maintained.

If as we age we experience both role loss and role changes then we should expect that the social structure of our society (its pattern of social organization) will reflect these facts. Social gerontologists have described the unique ways in which the elderly fit into the structures of society in relationship to the family, to the occupational and economic structure, and to the community, including such community-based services as housing, health-care, and voluntary organizations. The relationship of the aged to each of these social structures changes, and findings emphasize decline, weakening bonds, and increasing dependence in regard to them as we age.

Family Relationships.   One of the important elements of the social organization of any society is its institutions. A society's *institutions* are its arrangements of human effort to provide mechanisms to deal with issues such as mating, care for the young, education, socialization, production, distribution and consumption of goods, and so on.

The *family* is an institution set up to deal with the issues of procreation, legitimate sexual access between adults, caring for the young, socialization, consumption of goods, to some degree the production of goods (as in farming families), and much early education. As such it is extremely important in integrating the individual into the society (Streib and Thompson, 1960), and dislocation from the family would, therefore, contribute greatly to the isolation of an individual from many of his or her normal societal roles. We will want to examine how such a dislocation occurs among the elderly.

Social gerontology has focused on the changes in the family that have contributed to the loss of roles and isolation that the elderly suffer. One such notion of family changes has been the traditional notion of how a family changes as it goes through a sort of cycle with its aging members. This cycle—childhood to adolescence to courtship to marriage to parenthood to grandparenthood to widow or widower— has been described in a number of forms (for example, Duvall, 1971). Here one sees the progression of family memberships in one person's life as he or she moves from the family of orientation (the family in which one was raised) to the family of procreation (the family in which one is the parent). The family has also been seen as having changed in its structure as Western societies have become industrialized. As a result of the change in the structure of society, it has been suggested by sociologists such as Goode (1964) and Zelditch (1964) that extended families (those with several generations living in the same household) become too cumbersome for the highly mobile type of life which people live in the new organization of society. Thus the extended family is replaced by the nuclear family, in which only parents and their children live in the same household.

Such a change in the structure of the family would certainly have severe consequences for the social connectedness of the elderly. Koller (1968: 16) notes that "the comparative isolation of the elderly—stems in large measure from an evolving family pattern that has no place for older persons.'' Social gerontology has traced the way increasing pressures for individual mobility and achievement that came with industrialization made older family members less and less important to their children's success (Streib and Thompson, 1960) and therefore less central to the family. Theorists have differed as to the degree of isolation of the nuclear family from their families of orientation. Parsons (1959) suggests that the nuclear family is quite isolated, while Sussman and Burchinal (1962) argue that nuclear families are linked by exchanges of services both horizontally (to other similar families) and vertically (to their own parents). More recently Fischer (1977) has traced the history of the relationship between the family and the elderly claiming that there has never been an extended family in America, and that the resulting disengagement of the elderly from their own family of orientation has been with us since before industrialization.

Other influences on the relationships of the elderly to their families have been studied by social gerontologists. For example, Shanas (1968) has shown that social class is related to the living arrangements a family will create with its older members, with middle-class white collar adults most likely to live apart from their grown children. Other factors studied include the values held by the families (Kerckhoff, 1964). This refers primarily to the type of family living arrangement one wishes to have, and the influences of retirement, grandparenthood, and widow or widower status on the relationship of the elderly to the rest of their family. Decline in care for the elderly by their families has also been attributed to demographic changes, changes in women's social roles, and to changes in the economy (Treas, 1977). In addition, although the bulk of these studies focus on the relationships between the elderly and the families of their children, some work has been done in studying the marriages of older persons as families in their own right. Here the emphasis is on such factors as numbers and types of friends and neighbors (Riley and Foner, 1968), retirement (Kerckhoff, 1964), and death of a spouse and illness (Troll, 1971).

In these studies the emphasis is on discovering the degree of role loss, or as it is often called, societal disengagement, that the older person suffers as a result of the breakup of the extended family. When a person retires from his or her occupation, the family becomes increasingly important for the connection of the individual to the social network. To the extent that the family cannot serve this need, the older person will be increasingly isolated.

The Occupational and Economic Structures.   Our social well-being is intimately connected with our occupational and economic situations. Americans value wealth, power and/or status, and the work ethic—values most often expressed in a job and through the income derived from it. Much of our sense of self-worth and autonomy and many of our social contacts are also job related.

In less industrialized societies retirement from work may be less significant considering the importance that kinship, religious ties, and land holdings could continue to have for the individual. However, in the high-energy (Cottrell, 1955) technologies—those depending upon power converters like steam or electricity rather than animals or wind—of our modern societies the premiums on flexibility, mobility, recent job training, and complexity of organization seem to conspire against the continuation of the elderly in the work force. These societies also put such stress on individual achievement characteristics over ascribed ones, such as kinship, that a person's retirement is unlikely to be compensated for by other social ties (for example, Streib and Schneider, 1971).

How does retirement affect economic well-being and self-perception? Research by social gerontologists into retirement has focused on who retires, how they justify retirement, the impact of retirement on income and health, how the retiree adapts to retirement, society's attitudes toward retirement and the retiree, and so on.

Research on how one adapts to retirement has identified a number of factors believed to be important in this adjustment, such as personality, preparation for retirement, and attitude toward retirement. Reichard, Livson, and Petersen (1968) conclude that the personality of the retiree has an important effect on whether a person grows old successfully. The three well-adjusted types identified were:

> Mature—"relatively free of neurotic conflict, they were able to accept themselves realistically"
>
> "Rocking chair"—generally passive—"welcomed the opportunity to be free of responsibility and to indulge the passive needs of old age"
>
> "Armored"—"their strong defenses protected them from their fear of growing old" (Reichard, Livson, and Petersen, 1968: 178).

The poorly adjusted personalities were also named. The "angry men" were bitter about their failures and unable to accept growing old, blaming others for their condition. "Self-haters," like "angry men," were bitter about their failures and filled with resentment but tended to blame themselves rather than others for their condition.

Degree of preparation has been found to be associated with favorable attitude toward retirement (Greene and others, 1969), and, in turn, a favorable attitude toward retirement has been shown to be associated with personal adjustment to retirement (Thompson, Streib, and Kosa, 1960).

Others have studied the impact of retirement on income and the general financial condition of the retiree, on health and general life satisfaction, on self-esteem and on social isolation versus social participation.

The results of this research show retirement to have both negative and positive influences on the retiree. According to Streib and Schneider (1971: 80), "The social gerontological literature recognizes the drastic effects of retirement on the retiree's economic situation. A reduction of income in retirement is practically universal." However, both Streib and Schneider (1971) and Cottrell and Atchley (1969) find that retirement does not adversely affect self-esteem.

While Cottrell and Atchley's (1969) research finds that retirement most often produces no change in social participation (sometimes even increasing it), Rosenberg (1970) finds that retirement tends to increase social isolation among working class retirees. Bengtson's (1969) research suggests that retirement produces differing levels of role activity after retirement depending on nationality and the relationship of the activity to familial, organizational, or informal settings.

This mixture of negative and positive influences may be attributed to the tendency of this research to combine in samples those who have retired voluntarily with those who have been forced to retire. Miller (1965) suggests that among those who have involuntarily retired, the leisure such people "enjoy" is not the type we generally consider worthwhile. This type of leisure is generally a source of embarrassment for the involuntarily retired person. It is this sort of problem which has prompted a good deal of discussion of compulsory versus flexible (voluntary up to a point) retirement (Palmore, 1972).

The relationship of the elderly to the economic structure is very much related to their position in the work force. If one can predict that a worker will be retired at age 65, it is also possible to predict how many jobs will be available to other workers, and when. In addition replacement workers are usually a cheaper labor supply than a pool of older workers who have earned seniority, promotions, and many fringe benefits. These considerations and others have resulted in the institutionalization of retirement from the work force and in intergenerational conflict centered in the use of forced retirement to balance and control job supply and demand.

The relationship of the elderly to the economic structure is also a matter of the needs for services and goods that are peculiar to the elderly because of the dependent situation in which they have been put. For example, the use of medical and other health services by the elderly and their need for public transportation in the concentrated urban population centers make them consumers of services that are rather expensive to support and that traditionally are not self-sufficient. (Hospitals and mass transit systems habitually lose money in the big American cities.)

Beyond the economics of the aged as workers, we must look at their roles as investors and/or dependents in the economy. A wealthy older population would be a source of investment funds and a market for consumption, while a poor older population (deriving the bulk of its income from other than earned income sources) would influence the economic structure by demanding sevices beyond their ability to pay for them. The research of Kreps (1963 and 1966) and others (for example, Schulz, 1976) has highlighted these issues.

The economic impacts of aging are extremely wide ranging. Retirement generally halves older people's incomes, changing their buying patterns and increasing their dependence on public programs. Sometimes the elderly become totally dependent on government programs for income, housing, food, medical care, transportation, and so on, thereby losing many of their social connections—a process that can be seen as a measurement of the social aging process. Schulz asks whether enough is being done for the elderly or whether in fact enough can be done, given the burden of such programs on the economy. He notes that some have thought too much has been done, since the cost of programs benefiting the aged has increased more rapidly than that of programs benefiting any other group; the costs are also being borne by an increasingly burdened group of younger providers.

The Community.   The community is a third very important structure for the integration of individuals into the larger social order. Sociologists have treated the concept as having two elements: *territoriality,* or the physical boundaries in which interactions between a group of people commonly take place and *cohesiveness,* or the feeling of belonging which is associated with such a community by its members. The relationship between family and community is often quite close. However, although the family and the community are often interrelated, communities do involve an individual in organizations and activities *independently* of that person's family membership. It is this capacity that has interested social gerontologists.

Growing up in a community normally involves a person in its school system, its government, and its various voluntary associations such as religious and civic groups. While one's children may move away to start their own families, the ties to the community built over a lifetime remain. Little work has been done on the way participation in local politics helps integrate the older person into the community. However, some research has focused on voluntary association and on the community as a conduit for services to the elderly.

Voluntary Associations. Rose (1960: 670) reports that a number of studies " . . . generally show that social participation declines at the later ages despite the increased leisure time following upon retirement." Some of the factors suggested as influencing the participation of the elderly in voluntary associations are health (Atchley, 1977), socioeconomic status (Uzzell, 1953), retirement (Cottrell and Atchley, 1969), and transportation (Cutler, 1974).

Religion has been studied as a type of association of particular importance to the elderly. According to Maves (1960: 709), "religion has a relation to aging because it involves a response to the experience of aging, change, loss, and death. It involves a concern to find the ultimate meaning in these processes and to ascertain the significance of human life." In addition, religion may be of importance in its ability to provide a community tie for older people (Atchley, 1977), and because it has provided many services for the elderly such as workshops, hobby groups, day centers, and even meal programs (Rose, 1960). Social gerontologists have studied the relationship between age and religious belief (Moberg, 1965) and between age and religious attendance (Orbach, 1961). Attendance has generally been found to increase up to age 50 and then to drop off slowly, and belief in religion is found generally to increase with age. To the extent that voluntary associations like religious groups become refuges for the aged, they seem to contribute to the isolation of the old from the rest of society.

Community-Based Services for the Elderly. The community has often been viewed as the setting in which those services needed by the elderly, such as housing, medical care, transportation, and other social services, are delivered. In this area social gerontology has focused on discovering the needs that the elderly have for these services, and the extent to which programs to satisfy these needs have been successful.

Housing needs of the elderly have already been indirectly discussed in the section on the family in terms of the tendency of newly married couples to move out of their parents' homes. This leaves the newly alone parents with a house that had to be big enough to raise a family, but that now may be too large and, under the restraints of fixed income, too expensive to maintain. Research (United States Senate Subcommittee on Housing for the Elderly, 1962; Vivrett, 1960) has noted the influence of increasing population, physical disabilities among the aged, economic restrictions brought on by retirement, and how the elderly prefer to live on the relationship between the aged and the housing market. For example, Shanas (1962) reports that only a very small percentage of elderly interviewed (less than 10 percent) would rather live in their children's home than in their own. Winiecke (1973: 305) on the other hand, finds that those elderly who prefer to live in housing for the elderly " . . . are renters who live in apartments, separate houses and hotel rooms. They are younger and live alone. . . . Many are bored and lonely and would prefer to live in a place where people are similar to themselves."

While most older persons would rather be independent, living either in their own homes or in apartments, they are often trapped in poor housing in urban areas or forced by failing health or by financial burdens to move into housing established for them. The tendency for the aged to live in age-segregated housing has been discovered to be especially prevalent in cities (Cowgill, 1978). A body of research has focused on the quality of this housing and on the satisfaction of the elderly with it. The types of housing studied have ranged from apartment buildings that happen to have only old persons living in them (Hochschild, 1973a), to trailer parks for the elderly (Hoyt, 1954), to retirement housing (Rosow, 1961), and to nursing homes and other long-term care facilities for the elderly (Townsend, 1971). In some of these the housing is found to be adequate, but many studies of housing for the elderly, especially those of nursing homes (Mendelson, 1974; Garvin and Burger, 1968), severely criticize the quality of medical care and the facilities themselves.

Agencies of the government such as the Department of Health, Education, and Welfare regularly evaluate the general health of the aged as compared with the health of the rest of the population, and medical journals in geriatric medicine and public health also publish evaluations of the relative health of older populations. This information is of concern to sociologists because physical or mental illness may impair one's ability to interact in social settings and thus cause symptoms of sociological aging like role loss and isolation. Thus, given these health problems, gerontologists have also studied the availability in the community of health services for the elderly. Albert and Zarit (1977) conclude that the economic problems of the aged such as forced retirement and social security policies have contributed to the inadequacy of the health care the aged receive, and studies of national medical programs for the aged such as Medicare and Medicaid (which deals with health services for the poor, regardless of age) have noted the costs of these programs in both money and demands on the medical services used (Davis, 1973).

After retirement or when a spouse dies, older people become dependent on savings, private pension plans, or social security. Their incomes, and therefore their standards of living, generally decline severely, especially during inflationary times. Although Medicare and, in part, Medicaid were intended to protect the elderly from rising medical costs, these benefits have proven inadequate for medical care in a number of areas, including psychiatric, nursing home, dental, rehabilitative, and other services, especially when compared with the private care we buy as independent, income-earning members of society. These programs are also extremely expensive to support.

Research into nursing home health care (Mendelson, 1974; Garvin and Burger, 1968) has noted the economic, social (generally family centered), physiological and psychological circumstances that lead the aged to enter nursing homes or other long-term health care facilities for the aged. This type of institutionalization is the ultimate isolation from social relationships, with death being the almost inevitable result. In fact, Lynch (1977) has suggested that loneliness such as that experienced by the aged in nursing homes may in fact cause illness and death in an all too real interpretation of the fanciful image of dying of a broken heart.

In sum, social gerontology has suggested that as we age, our connections with the social groups around us diminish. We experience role losses analogous to the physical and psychological deterioration in other facets of our lives. Among the areas in which social gerontology has found decline in our social bonds are:

1. Loss of family bonds with the decline of the extended family, and breakup of the marriage due to the death of one's mate;
2. Loss of one's occupational roles (whether job or home centered), and the loss of the associations dependent upon them;
3. Loss of community leadership and involvement replaced by dependence upon the community as a conduit for services;
4. Loss of control over one's economic well-being. This may lead to loss of the independent household and a move into segregated housing for the elderly. Many other forms of dependence flow from this particular loss;

5. Loss of control over one's own life and decisions, often relinquishing choices to one's children or to social welfare professionals;
6. Loss of interaction with young persons in general;
7. Loss of future time orientation; and
8. Loss of one's instrumental value in the society.

Maintaining the Age-Related Societal Relationships

The aged are not unique in having a particular relationship to the structure of society; sociologists have described such relationships in terms of race, class, sex, and urbanism as well. Each group is oriented to the larger society in special ways that reflect not only the characteristics of the group in question, but characteristics of the society as well. What all have in common, however, is that if the relationship to the society is to be relatively stable, then it must be maintained by some mechanism or mechanisms. How are the relationships between the aged and the structures of society maintained?

By the process of socialization individuals come to learn the values and appropriate behaviors of their society, and to internalize them. Although socialization is unique for any individual, the shared beliefs of the society come to be reflected in the way society's members are socialized. To the extent that the essential values of a culture are transmitted to large numbers of its members, that culture is maintained or perpetuated.

The abstract, underlying values of a culture, such as progress, science, the future, individualism, freedom and justice, are expressed on the everyday level by *norms,* rules of behavior that tell people what is expected of them and what is correct to do. That young married couples in American culture usually wish to move into their own home as soon as possible is normative behavior and expresses the underlying cultural values of independence, planning for the future, and mobility. Similarly, the tendency of parents to help their married children in their careers and family finances (Sussman and Burchinal, 1962) is a norm that expresses the way we value kinship within the family structure.

In this way socialization to the values and norms of our culture tends to perpetuate the existing relationships of the elderly to the structures of the society. The elements of the culture that most directly influence the place of the elderly in the society are those which make up what has been called the "youth culture." Here the emphasis is on those norms for behavior that favor youth and make them central to the functioning of society. These are reflected in ideas about attractiveness, in our quest for speed and efficiency, in our interest in athletic rather than sedentary pastimes, the favoring of "new" ideas, fashions, and so on.

Not only are there norms for behavior by the young, but age norms that apply to various stages of life (Atchley, 1975). They are maintained by socialization and are held by members of the society for the actions of an individual, and by the individual for his or her own behavior. Thus, attitudes towards the elderly and expectations for their behavior are found to be similar among the old and the young (McTavish, 1971).

Research into the way socialization is related to aging has not, however, focused on the way age norms have maintained the existing age-related structures of society. Rather it has tended to describe how aging individuals prepare themselves for old age by the process of adult, or *anticipatory socialization* (Atchley, 1977)—the process whereby we learn what behavior is expected in a new role before we actually occupy that role. Sociologists recognize that since our world is constantly changing we must adapt to those changes by continuing socialization as adults. Among the changes that we can expect in our lives are changes in our life-cycle such as from single to married status and from that of worker to retired person.

Rosow (1974) suggests that while the norms for behavior at most stages of life are strong and positive (for example the norms for work and raising a family during young to middle adulthood), the norms for old age are weak and negative. He claims the norms for old age cluster about an undesirable dependency on others and are lacking in specific guides or "role content and activity—in a word, what older people should do with their available time and energy and how they should shape their lives" (Rosow, 1974: 69). Thus, the possibilities for anticipatory socialization to old age are greatly reduced since the motivation to do so is diminished by both the negative character of norms for the aged and by their lack of clarity, what another researcher, Burgess (1960), has called adapting to a roleless role.

A separate segment of the research by social gerontologists into socialization focuses on attitudes held by the elderly. This literature traces the changes in attitude that accompany aging and that are accomplished by adult socialization. As examples this research has described the attitudes of the elderly

1. Towards institutions (Riley and Foner, 1968),
2. Towards minorities (Thune, 1967),
3. Towards youth (Cryns and Monk, 1973),

4. Towards death (Riley and Foner, 1968),
5. Towards crime (Harris, 1975),
   and so on.

One of the problems of such studies is that the elderly are extremely heterogeneous. It is as difficult to characterize their attitudes as those of young or middle-aged people. But more importantly, by focusing on the attitudes of the elderly we only obscure a very important assumption underlying such research. The choice by gerontologists of what, or whom, to study is much more revealing than their findings.

In an effort to understand aging, gerontologists have focused almost exclusively on the old. Their assumption is that the process and problems of aging are rooted in the characteristics of the aging individual. Accordingly, the evidence is seen in physiological, psychological, and social changes, including, of course, the attitude changes that accompany aging. This assumption will be examined in the next chapter.

Summary

This chapter has presented a look at some of the research produced in the three main fields of gerontology—the physiology, psychology, and sociology of aging.

Research in the physiology of aging has tended to discover loss or reduction in various physical functions of the body—resulting in higher death rates and more serious illness among the elderly than in the rest of the population and in changes in the cosmetic appearance of the body. Declines in the effectiveness of operation of various of the body's systems, especially the circulatory and nervous systems, were described. Various theories of physiological aging were presented: a "biological clock" model; a "wear-and-tear" model; a waste-products model; a proposal that the stiffening of connective collagen is the cause of aging; that the immune system wears down and thus reduces our ability to resist disease; and that mutations within the body's cells disrupt the operation of the organism either by excessive mutation or by triggering an autoimmune response within the body.

The review of the literature in the psychology of aging traced the influence of aging on the sensory and perceptual processes, psychomotor performance, on the cognitive processes, on drives and motives, and on personality. In many cases, results were either unclear or contradictory. Yet, the theme of loss of capacity and overall decline that appeared in the literature of the physiology of aging, seems to occur in the psychology of aging as well.

The review of the research in sociological aging dealt with descriptions in the literature of the relationships between the aged and the rest of society, and the consequences of such relationships—isolation, economic dependence, role loss—and with the relationships between the elderly and such specific societal structures as the family, the community, and the economy. The literature also described some of the mechanisms, such as socialization, whereby these relationships have been maintained.

Chapter Two

Blaming the Aged

Chapter One presented an overview of some of the research in gerontology. How has this research shaped our understanding of the process of aging? Are we better able to control or minimize the problems associated with aging and suffered by the aged? What sorts of programs have been developed out of this research and have they been effective? Is there some unifying theme that characterizes this literature and contributes to the understanding of aging as a process? This chapter will attempt to evaluate the answers given to these questions by the researchers in the field of gerontology.

The investigation of aging by gerontologists has been conducted at the level of the individual, and if there is one unifying theme in this research and theory building, it is that *aging* is something that *happens to individuals*. It is seen as occurring in skin, muscles, and blood vessels, in changes in abilities to think, remember, perceive, and innovate. It is even charted in withdrawal from old associations such as the family, and in disengagement from society, as in retirement.

This is a perspective that blames the aged for the problems they suffer. Rather than focusing on the *social* forces that make old age a difficult, even dreaded stage of life, we have blamed biology or the ravages of time. The only place where such ravages of time are apparent is in the aged themselves, and the more we investigate them, the more it *looks* as if the aged display on their faces and in their bodies the symptoms and causes of their difficulties.

Since the research conducted by scientists is intimately related to the theories and assumptions that dominate their disciplines, it is reasonable to guess that the theories in gerontology reflect concern with characteristics of the aged, a concern apparent in the specific questions researchers have asked. As we saw in Chapter One, the theories of aging in physiological and psychological research clearly focus on characteristics of the aged, and social gerontology, the discipline with the greatest potential for studying elements of aging *other than* characteristics of the aged, has also tended to focus on characteristics of the old in both its research and theories. The result of research in all three of these areas has been to tacitly blame the aged for their own problems—to blame the victim (Ryan, 1971).

Blaming the Victim

Victim-blaming is the tendency when examining a social problem to attribute that problem to the characteristics of the people who are its victims. For example, Ryan (1971) notes the way Daniel P. Moynihan's (1965) study of the black family attributes the bulk of the deprivations suffered by blacks in America to the characteristics of blacks. In this case, Moynihan claims that the breakdown in the black family, recognizable in the absence of the father and the dominance of the mother, has serious consequences for the children of such families. The child, provided with an inadequate role model (the failed father) and typically dependent on relief and other services beyond the family, becomes "so damaged by their family experience that they are unable to profit from educational and employment opportunities" (Ryan, 1971: 64). Poorly equipped to take advantage of what scant opportunities are available, the child is presumed to have the seeds of failure in his or her own character. Any role that the rest of the society may play in denying both family and child equal opportunities in a variety of areas is not considered.

Similarly, Oscar Lewis (1966) in studying the poor has found what he terms the "culture of poverty." His analysis contends that a child of poverty not only experiences deprivations in terms of poor education and lack of adequate family life or role models, but such deprivations become a way of life. The life of poverty among poor people supposedly develops into a subculture of poverty that " . . . tends to perpetuate itself. By the time slum children are six or seven they have usually absorbed the basic attitudes and values of their subculture. Thereafter, they are psychologically unready to take full advantage of changing conditions or improving opportunities that may develop in their life time" (Lewis, 1966: 7). This subculture of the poor is assumed to be responsible for the sufferings of the poor; it is assumed to be the cause of the problem itself.

Take the instance of a poor child who lives in an urban slum.

The education, clothing, food, and other elements necessary to his success in later life are denied him by the structure of the society in which he lives. But the victim-blamers contend that his inability to succeed is due to those individual characteristics that were caused by these "cultural deprivations." The solution they pose is to eliminate those unfortunate characteristics by programs that educate the poor child, thus bringing his or her values and abilities more in line with those of the rest of the society in which he or she will compete.

The flaw in these arguments and solutions is in treating the symptoms of the discriminations rather than the discriminations themselves. If the structure that allows, or even depends upon, such discriminations were to be changed, the symptoms would also decline. In the absence of changes to the larger system, poverty will continue, and the victim-blamers will continue to advocate remedial intervention into the lives of the poor. It is not being suggested here that those who suffer the symptoms of poverty not be aided; however, to the extent that such aid makes us believe that the problems are being dealt with we may neglect to act on the root causes, and thus perpetuate them.

Blaming the victim for the problem he or she suffers is merely a matter of identifying those characteristics which distinguish that individual from the rest of the population and proposing how the problem may result from them. In the example of the culture of poverty (often interchangeable with the problems of racial minority groups), it is primarily the lack of middle class values that are presumed to keep the poor person from climbing out of the slums. Inability to delay gratification, lack of respect for the value of education, and lack of ambition are identified as the causes of the problem. If only the proper values could be instilled in the poor they would obviously become successful, and there would be no problem. Programs of counseling, education, incentives to work, disincentives to go on welfare, and so on continue to be advocated in spite of the failure of all these programs to reduce the levels of poverty or the suffering it causes.

Ryan (1971: 8) describes the system of blaming the victim: "First, identify a social problem. Second, study those affected by the problem and discover in what ways they are different from the rest of us as a consequence of deprivation and injustice. Third, define the differences as the cause of the social problem itself. Finally, of course, assign a government bureaucrat to invent a humanitarian action program to correct the differences." Ryan's acid use of the word "humanitarian" suggests the gap between the harsh reality of blaming the victim and the reputation for compassion enjoyed by those who advocate programs to aid the victims. They seem unwilling to entertain the possibility that the problems that poor people and other groups suffer are primarily the result of larger circumstances surrounding the victims. By reason of their majority-group membership and influence in policy making and program planning, the victim-blamers have more control over social circumstances than do the victims, but acknowledging that social problems may be the result of one's own actions or the actions of one's peers would be painful. It might even result in changes in the very system that provides majority-group members with a relatively comfortable style of life.

If poverty and other forms of deprivation do indeed result from racism, discrimination, and the competitiveness of our social and economic order, then surely the more powerful groups in society are more to blame for these problems than are the victims. But blaming the victim not only allows one to avoid feelings of guilt, it allows also feelings of "good will" toward those less fortunate. These feelings are reinforced by the establishment of programs to "help" such victims by correcting those characteristics which make them incapable of competing.

Blaming the victim is not confined to dealing with social problems such as poverty and racial conflict. The problem of criminal behavior is often attributed to the flawed characteristics of the criminal, and so we attempt to "rehabilitate" the criminal. The problem of divorce is often discovered in the values and beliefs of those whose marriages fail, and so counseling is suggested for them. The inability to read well is attributed to the student's lack of motivation or poor diet, and so programs to feed and motivate are developed. Ryan even notes that lead-paint poisoning of babies has been blamed on parents who allow their children to eat the paint, rather than on landlords who will not spend the money to get rid of the paint. The program begun to alleviate the problem does not repaint apartments, it educates mothers to keep their children from eating the paint (Ryan, 1971).

Exceptionalist and Universalistic Views of Social Problems

Frequently, we see that the programs designed to deal with social problems call for resocialization of the victim so that the characteristics he or she has that "caused" the problem can be eradicated. Ryan calls this type of program exceptionalist. "The exceptionalist viewpoint is reflected in arrangements that are private, voluntary, remedial, special, local, and exclusive. . . . The problems are unusual, even unique, they are exceptions to the rule" (Ryan, 1971: 16–17).

The perception of problems as special, as exceptions to the rule, is very much a part of our approach to order and disorder. We tend to see order as normal, and disruption (and sometimes even change) in that order as abnormal or problematic. Thus, any problem, since it is merely an abnormality, a temporary hitch in the smooth operation of an essentially balanced system, can be dealt with as a special case. We need not tamper with the essential structure of the larger system. Thus, a criminal is sent to prison for deviant behavior in hopes of resocializing him or her. If the effort is judged successful, a return to society is likely. This is an exceptionalist solution. The cause of the disruptive criminal behavior is assumed to be in the individual rather than in the structure of society or in some system larger than the individual, so no changes in the system are judged necessary.

By contrast, the belief that problems stem from societal arrangements calls for what Ryan has termed a universalistic approach. This " . . . is reflected in arrangements that are public, legislated, promotive or preventive, general, national and inclusive" (Ryan, 1971: 17). Universalistic programs call for changes in the organization of society so that conditions which create problems are eliminated. Such programs acknowledge that social problems may be rooted in the very structure of a society; they deny that problems are inevitably extrasystematic. To illustrate, resocialization is exceptionalist, but the provision of jobs and income (or the elimination of job discrimination) for people who might otherwise have to steal is universalistic. Besides usually costing more, universalistic solutions acknowledge that the causes of problems lie with the most advantaged members of society. An exceptionalist approach allows such blame to be avoided. As would be expected of a society that uses a victim-blaming approach in its study and treatment of aging, our programs for the elderly have been exceptionalist rather than universalistic. These programs will be more fully discussed in a subsequent section of this chapter.

Social Order and Social Problems

Earlier, it was suggested that we tend to view order as normal and disorder as abnormal. This was identified as one reason for the logic of blaming the victim rather than blaming the system surrounding the victim. If we assume that any system, whether physical, psychological, or social, tends towards balance or equilibrium, then any change in the balance of that system must come from outside its boundaries. To the extent that we believe such systems *should* be maintained as they are, then exceptionalist solutions seem not only appropriate, but inevitable.

As an illustration think about the way medicine is conducted and studied in our society. Historically, medicine has been seen as an intervening process; it deals with disruptions in the operation of the human system—with disorder. This approach has affected the structuring of medical research and the system of health care in our society. Since we treat illness, not health, our medical system is not one of health care but of disease care. It employs an exceptionalist approach. Medicine has been criticized for its emphasis on curing illness rather than preventing it as with health maintenance programs. (A similar characterization applies to the system of mental health in our society.)

Among sociologists the identification, analysis, and treatment of social problems is most directly influenced by the belief in the primacy of order. Since social order is a human construction (with variations between societies as to what is normal), any society may decide for itself what constitutes disorder. While in one society violence between individuals may be considered disruptive, in another, such behavior may be central to the accepted system of resolving intergroup disputes. In one society competitiveness may be considered unseemly and disruptive, while in another it may be considered an essential part of the structure of achievement and excellence. Social problems are only deemed social problems to the extent that they are so defined by the dominant forces in a society. Thus, Ryan (1971: 11–12) notes that, "before the 1930's, the most anti-Semitic German was unaware that Germany had a 'Jewish problem.' It took the Nazis to name the simple existence of Jews in the Third Reich as a social problem, and that act of definition helped to shape the final solution." Similarly, in our own society the roles of women and the elderly were not always considered problems although both issues existed long before they were discussed in texts on social problems (for example, Raab, 1973).

C. Wright Mills (1943) has described how the discussion of social problems by sociologists has reflected their concern for social order and resulted in exceptionalist approaches to problems. According to Mills (1943: 166), books on social problems present their findings in a "fragmentary way with scattered problems and facts of milieux, . . . not focused on larger stratifications or upon structured wholes." The bulk of their presentation seems merely informational. For example, in gerontology it has been suggested (Maddox and Wiley, 1977: 5) that " . . . the literature on aging as a social problem is largely descriptive and *atheoretical.* . . . " However, the underlying theme relating all the social problems they discuss is that these problems are aberrations—deviations from the essentially stable and desirable norms that comprise the dominant social structure. The stability and desirability of the system are assumed, and therefore, unexamined. "The basis of stability, order, and solidarity is not typically analyzed in these books, but a conception of such a basis is implicitly used and sanctioned, some normative conception of a socially healthy and stable organization is involved in the determination of pathological conditions" (Mills, 1943: 174).

Given that the social order as it appears in America is seen as synonymous with stability and normalcy, then social problems appear to us as deviations from that order. "Poverty is a problem in that it deviates from the standard of economic self-sufficiency; divorce is a problem because the family is supposed to remain intact; crime and delinquency are problematic insofar as they depart from the accepted moral and legal standards of the community" (Ryan, 1971: 12). If the stability of our normative order is paramount, then a view of deviation from it as pathological (with the disease rooted in the individual) is inevitable.[1]

Blaming the Aged

Ryan's description of how we blame the victim in our approach to social problems emphasizes the process whereby a group of people come to develop the traits that "cause" their problems. According to this view, through no fault of their own, members of one group or another suffer "involuntary neglect" (Kardiner, 1968) while growing up. As a result they are handicapped both emotionally and intellectually in facing the rigors of everyday life. That is why they are defined as failures, and failure is considered a social problem. Victim-blamers emphasize that such people are not born inferior, but that they are made inferior by circumstances.

Gerontologists have tended to take this perspective when studying the processes and problems of aging. In the literature of

[1]The concern among sociologists with order is deeply rooted in the origins of the sociological perspective. Sociology in the West can be traced to reactions to the upheavals accompanying what Robert Nisbet (1966) has called the "two revolutions," the industrial and democratic. The older order, characterized by aristocracy, land, kinship, the sacred and closed, relatively autonomous community gave way to the new secular, differentiated contract-based society. Sociology started as a search for what the loss of the old order might mean, and the possibilities for social stability in the new.

Despite sociology's reputation today as a source of liberal and radical thought, a number of critics continue to charge sociology with excessive conservatism, a system-maintaining defense of the order as it is (Gouldner, 1970).

gerontology, old people, like the poor, are described as having debilitating characteristics that cause being old to be a problem. While the
old are not accused of developing these unfortunate characteristics
intentionally (in fact, they are attributed to the most innocent of
causes, biology), they are nevertheless seen as the cause of the problems associated with advanced age.

For example, in rejecting the view that mandatory retirement
constitutes a form of discrimination against the elderly gerontologist
Gordon Streib (1976: 169) says " . . . over half of the persons who
retire say they are unable to work because of declining health. Thus,
most people are 'victims' of their own biology—not 'victims' of society." Clearly we cannot wish away that decline which accompanies
aging—some physical and psychological capacities do deteriorate.
However, at what rate would they decline if the treatment of old age in
our society were different? How could the structure of our society be
changed so that it minimizes the consequences of these losses? What
gains in capacity with advancing years are masked by the generalized
expectations of losses, and what losses are imagined where they do not
actually exist?

We have seen that gerontology tends to treat aging as an independent variable (assumed cause), something that shapes the way we
live our later lives. We should also see aging as an important dependent
variable (assumed effect), the result of the structure of the complex
society in which we live.

The preceding chapter has outlined the research and theorizing
that takes aging as an independent variable. To begin with, there are
the findings of decline in physiological capacity. When people cannot
move as well or as quickly as they once did, they have problems
operating in the everyday world. Losses in sight and hearing are terri-
bly damaging to our ability to manage for ourselves. Higher rates of
serious illness make us dependent upon medical services and devour
our time and energies just in staying alive. Long-term but less life-
threatening illness becomes a nagging partner in daily activities, rob-
bing us of our ability to concentrate well or to enjoy what we can
actually accomplish. Such physical deterioration may deprive us of the
opportunity to be gainfully employed, either because we are actually
unable to do a job or because an employer is afraid we may be too slow.
In either case, loss of employment affects our sense of independence
and well-being.

Findings of psychological deterioration describe the same
types of problems. Losses in sensory capacity limit both the enjoyment
and performance of the activities of the elderly. Psychomotor perfor-

mance may decline, influencing mobility (as in driving a car) and the ability to perform a job. Changes in drives and motivation have serious consequences for health and the ability to accomplish what one wishes. A reputation for lowered intelligence, problem-solving ability, and creativity may contribute to feelings of uselessness, as one is consulted less frequently for advice and aid. In addition, these losses or the expectation of them, may be responsible for actual loss of valuable roles as one is isolated from those life-long relationships which depend upon these abilities.

We cannot say to what extent the findings of decline are the result of age itself, and to what extent the result of expectation of such loss. For example, Cottrell (1974) suggests that although the tendency of old people to eat less has been attributed to loss of appetite (a drive), they are found to be quite willing to eat well if their food is prepared decently and they have some company at meals. Similarly, the aged have the reputation of being inflexible, poor at job performance, and lower in intelligence than younger people—in spite of evidence that strongly contradicts these images (see Chapter Three). They are denied jobs or retired from jobs they hold for fear they will become inflexible, poor workers, and less intelligent.

Research findings in the physiology and psychology of aging are used in the theories, research, and programs that blame the victim. For example, the findings of physiological decline form the basis of *disengagement theory,* a major social theory of aging that takes a victim-blaming approach. It suggests that inevitable physical decline requires that individuals and society mutually withdraw in advance of this decline, to the supposed benefit of both. Expectations of decline in psychological capacities such as in psychomotor speed and accuracy and in intelligence and memory have been used to justify the removal of individuals from their jobs by legal, mandatory retirement. The resulting isolation and ill health are among the major problems suffered by the aged.

The critical factor in the determination of these victim-blaming perspectives on the aged and aging has been the choice of what, or who, to study—a process Ryan calls "savage discovery." Certainly the biological study of human disease does not automatically blame the victim, nor does the study of human psyche. *However, when physiologists study the physical characteristics of blacks, or psychologists study their temperaments or intelligence levels, it is implied that the characteristics of blacks have something to do with their problems, or may even have caused them.* Similarly, by studying the characteristics of the aged it is implied that their problems are the result of their

failings. *Physiologists and psychologists could well have chosen to study the young or the middle-aged in society in order to discover the causes of the problems associated with aging. They chose, however, to single out the aged for study, and by so doing have blamed the old for their problems, even before their first research findings were reported.*
Let us look at some of the theories and research of social gerontology.

Disengagement Theory

Social gerontological theory has been dominated for the last 15 or so years by a debate between disengagement theory and various forms of what has come to be called activity theory. The original name given by Cumming and Henry (1961) to the activity theory of aging was implicit theory, the idea that successful aging meant continuing middle-age life into one's later years. Continuity theory continued this emphasis—focusing on the maintenance into late life of one's lifestyles and commitments. Most recently this approach has been called activity theory and has focused on the maintenance of one's activity level from middle age on. Activity theory will be discussed later in this chapter.

Disengagement theory was proposed by Cumming and Henry (1961) largely in reaction to what they saw as the "implicit assumption" in previous gerontological research that happiness and success in old age are the result of continuing the activities and involvements of one's middle years without interruption. "In short, there appears to be a latent assumption that successful aging consists in being as much like a middle-aged person as possible" (Cumming and Henry, 1961: 18). According to disengagement theory, later life is different from the middle years and so a different style of life and level of social involvement apply.

Cumming and Henry suggested that "disengagement is an inevitable process in which many of the relationships between a person and other members of society are severed, and those remaining are altered in quality" (1961: 211). The presumed inevitability of this process is laid at the door of biology. "The society and the individual prepare in advance for the ultimate 'disengagement' of incurable, incapacitating disease and death by an inevitable, gradual and mutually satisfying process of disengagement from society" (Rose, 1964: 46). In order to accomplish this disengagement, starting in middle age the individual gradually is separated from many of his or her former roles systematically reducing the level of social interaction. This process is said to be normal and functional for both the society and the individual. For example, the society, presumably to avoid the disruption of having its fully engaged members dying or becoming inefficient "on the job," retires them, and the retired individual, having been freed of an encumbering tie, is now free to complete disengagement in other areas of life and to move towards death. Disengagement theory is a functionalist theory in that it assumes that society is a system in balance that seeks stability or equilibrium. Disengagement is a process that contributes to that equilibrium by making the exit of its members predictable, and therefore less disruptive. Like other processes that are functional for society, disengagement has become institutionalized as in laws allowing for mandatory retirement.

Since disengagement is proposed as a mutual process, the theory allows for two types of disengagement, societal and individual. Societal disengagement is evident in the retreat of the environment from the individual as in the departure of one's children from the family, retirement from the occupation, and possibly the deaths of spouse, friends, and relatives. Individual disengagement appears in the loss of many of an individual's contacts and job-related activities, and the turning of one's attention toward internal, personal, rather than external, concerns.[2]

According to disengagement theory, when the individual and society are mutually engaged (the individual and society both desiring such involvement), balance is maintained. Similarly, when both society and the individual wish to disengage, balance exists. The problems occur when either the individual wishes to remain engaged and the society does not or the individual wishes to disengage but the society does not wish him or her to do so. As would be predicted in a struggle between individual and societal forces, Cumming and Henry (1961: 215) suggest that society will prevail in either situation—"when the individual is ready [to disengage] and society is not, . . . usually engagement continues. When society is ready and the individual is not, the result of the disjunction is usually disengagement."

---

[2]Disengagement theory was preceded by Phillips' (1957) proposal of role theory. This approach to aging is quite similar to the individual disengagement component of the theory of disengagement. It suggests that sociological aging is largely the result of the adjustments aged people must make to "conditions that are not generally characteristic of other stages of life, namely, the increased probability of illness and impending death" (Phillips, 1957: 212). This entails "the relinquishment of social relationships and roles typical of adulthood, and the acceptance of social relationships and roles typical of the later years" (Phillips, 1957: 212). Disengagement theory differs from role theory in its emphasis on the functional nature of disengagement for both the society and the individual, and in its suggestion that disengagement involves mutual disengagement of society and the individual from one another.

The theory of disengagement has prompted a great deal of response since its original publication. In 1963 Cumming added to the theory an elaboration of how differences in character may contribute to variations in the rate and style of individual disengagement. At about the same time, the original theory's coauthor, Henry (1964) attributed the processes of engagement and disengagement to psychological rather than sociological mechanisms. These adjustments to the original theory are interesting in that they place added emphasis on the characteristics of the individual (rather than on characteristics of the society) as determinants of disengagement.

Some Criticisms and Refinements of Disengagement Theory

Research conducted to test some of the predictions of disengagement theory has developed mixed and contradictory findings. While Newell's (1961) finding of role loss with increasing age supports the theory, others (Cottrell and Atchley, 1969; Streib and Schneider, 1971) have found that after retirement, individuals are as likely to gain as to lose social roles. More recently, Mindel and Vaughan (1978) have found that the elderly may disengage vis-à-vis organizations but remain engaged nonorganizationally. In addition, some research has suggested that disengagement often reflects the lack of opportunity for continued engagement rather than the desire to disengage (Carp, 1968; Roman and Taietz, 1967). For example, Roman and Taietz's (1967) research found that college professors, given the opportunity to do so, preferred to remain engaged in their professions via the emeritus position rather than to retire entirely as disengagement theory might predict.

Other critics of disengagement theory have focused on the accuracy of its predictions. For example, some researchers have found that continued activity (Havighurst, 1968a) or re-engagement (Jacobs and Vinick, 1977) are more likely to be satisfying for the older individual than disengagement. Others have criticized disengagement theory on nonempirical bases, such as Rose's (1964) accusation that disengagement theory is a functionalist theory that overemphasizes the stability and appropriateness of the age structure as it is, or Hochschild's (1975) suggestion that the very logic of disengagement theory is faulty, including an "escape clause" that makes disproving the theory impossible.

A number of other studies while not directly in response to disengagement theory have focused on the way individuals adjust to old age; that is to say, how they manage to deal with their own individual disengagement (George and Maddox, 1977). Among the techniques of adaptation identified by this research have been

1. substitution of new activities for lost ones (Havighurst, 1963),
2. emphasis by the individual on a particular style of life such as living
   alone or focus on a marriage that works well given the circumstances of a disengaging person (Williams and Wirths, 1965), and
3. adaptation to the changing circumstances (societal demands) that
   aging brings to bear on the individual; such adaptations may include redefining one's abilities, physical and social space, self-
   evaluation processes, values, goals, and sources of satisfaction.
                                              (Clark and Anderson, 1967)

Disengagement Theory and Victim-Blaming

A further criticism of disengagement theory is that it is a perspective that blames the aged for their own condition. At first glance
the theory of disengagement seems to have great potential for focusing
on socioenvironmental influences on the process of aging, rather than
on the aging person. After all, its formulators, Cumming and Henry
(1961) claim that both the individual *and* the social system are benefited by the process of disengagement. That is, the social system benefits
from the removal of individuals who might disrupt its smooth operation
by becoming ill or dying while still fully engaged, and the individual is
freed to come to terms with his or her dying. But attention to the social
system aspects of disengagement should actually outweigh concern
with individual disengagement because as we have previously noted
the authors acknowledged the power of society to impress on the individual its own desires as to the timing of one's disengagement. The
theory of disengagement could have concerned itself with those aspects of the social system which are disrupted by the failure of individuals to disengage and focused on how such systems bring to bear
pressures to disengage. Had it done so, disengagement theory could
not be accused of having blamed the victim. Instead, the emphasis of
disengagement theory has been on the characteristics of *individual*
disengagement.

Instead of asking "How does the economic structure of the
society operate in such a way as to require the removal at age 65 or 70
of its workers?", disengagement theory asked how men as opposed to
women disengage from their social involvements. Instead of asking
"What are the mechanisms whereby one group in society serves its
interests at the cost of another group?", disengagement theory asked
how individuals adjust to role loss. Instead of asking "How is it that
one group in society, such as the aged, are chosen to be disengaged
rather than some other group, such as the rich?", disengagement
theory asked how disengagement relates to individual life-satisfaction.
The differences in the actual and theoretical questions shows how a

socioenvironmental approach differs from one that focuses on characteristics of the individual.

Borrowing from the findings in physiological and psychological research, disengagement theory assumes that individuals decline, using this as the starting point for the theory. Thus, individuals decline in the ability to operate in the everyday world so their continued engagement is presumed to be a threat to the equilibrium of the various social systems in which they are involved. Due to its basic assumptions, the disengagement theory must focus on the characteristics of the aged. This is quite similar to Ryan's (1971) discovery that the poverty of some people is blamed on their inability to delay gratification and their lack of a work ethic. It is their lack of *middle-class* attributes that causes the poor their problems, while among the aged, it is their lack of *middle-aged* attributes that causes their problems. The aged are seen as physically weaker and slower and lacking in the forward-looking, creative, flexible, and energetic outlooks that are necessary to full societal engagement.

From the acceptance of this underlying assumption, that the characteristics of the aged cause their own disengagement, flows a wealth of victim-blaming hypotheses and research. Most interestingly, it does not matter whether the research finds variations in adjustment to retirement, or variations in the dogmatism, rigidity, authoritarianism, voting behavior, psychosis, life-satisfaction, fear of death, desire to live alone, membership in voluntary associations, religiosity, loneliness, or even suicide rates among old people. It does not matter simply because all of these questions are focused on old people themselves. They ask how the old person adjusts to disengagement, how the old person reacts, how old age itself causes, or reacts to, disengagement.

As an example of this facet of disengagement theory, Cumming (1963), one of the coauthors of the original theory of disengagement, described how the temperament of a person might influence his or her style of disengagement from society. She suggested that "impingers" who " . . . will try to bring others' responses into line with his own sense of the appropriate relationships" are more likely to remain engaged in later life than will "selectors" who tend " . . . to wait for others to affirm his concept of himself" (Cumming, 1963: 379). As in most of the rest of the literature dealing with disengagement, the emphasis here is on the variety of ways individuals respond to pressures for disengagement, and on the characteristics of individuals that make disengagement necessary for their own well-being.

Disengagement theorists have tended not to look beyond the

individual in the search for the sources of the problems associated with aging because they have a functionalist view of the nature of social order. An analysis of a social problem that does not focus on characteristics of the victim must acknowledge that social problems can be rooted in the very structure of the social order—there is no other place to look. For disengagement theorists, this is not possible.

Disengagement Theory and the Functionalist Perspective

Disengagement theory is an example of functionalist theory in the style of its principal exponent, Talcott Parsons. Like other functionalist statements, disengagement theory rests on the assumption that society is a complex system of interdependent parts, which, as an overall system, tends toward stability or equilibrium. That is, societal structures are best understood in terms of how they, and the substructures of which they are built, tend towards balanced, stable systems of human interaction. According to Parsons, "since the structure of social systems consists in institutionalized normative culture, the 'maintenance' of these normative patterns is a basic reference point for analysing the *equilibrium* of the system" (Parsons, 1961: 37).

This concern with equilibrium and order causes functionalist theory to focus on relatively stable points of reference, or structural aspects of the system under study, in order to discover the processes whereby such structures are maintained. This is the primary emphasis of the structural-functional approach to social systems analyses. Since the social system is a system of action and its structural aspects are the relatively stable interactions of individuals around common norms, *the processes with which the functionalist becomes concerned are those which function to maintain a social structure.* On one level, these are the ways individuals come to be motivated to act in conformity with our normative standards. In the case of the behavior of older people, the issue becomes the discovery of those processes which cause individuals to *want* to disengage. This is presumed to be to the benefit of the equilibrium of the individual and of all involved social systems.

Structural functionalism posits *a strain towards order and equilibrium, and the social world is investigated for evidence of contribution to that order.* Thus, disengagement theory suggests how even so apparently disruptive a situation as withdrawal from life-long engagement in society may be seen as contributing to the equilibrium of both society and the disengaging individual.

A problem with this approach is that some individuals do not want to disengage and even more significantly, that old age is commonly treated as a social problem of some magnitude. How does Parsonian functionalism deal with what appears here to be evidence of system disruption? Parsons suggests the following:

> The functioning of a unit in an interaction system ultimately depends on the motivation of the individual actors participating in the unit. The "tension management" aspect of the pattern-maintenance sub-system concerns this motivation. The primary adaptive exigencies of this sub-system lie in those *personality* elements which maintain adequate motivation to conform with cultural values. The tension which is managed is individual motivation, in actual or potential conflicts with the fulfillment of behavior expectations in institutionally defined roles. Unless controlled or managed, such tension disorganizes the relevant unit and thereby interferes with its functioning in the system.
> (Parsons and Smelser, 1959: 134)

Notice that, for Parsons, pressures that result in disorganizing behavior are not the result of social processes; social processes are assumed to make only for patterned or stabilizing behaviors. Functionalism of this sort asserts that disruptions to a system must be introduced from *outside* that system, as in the faulty motivation of individuals to act out their roles properly. Such "flawed" motivations are deemed to be "tensions" that the system must "manage." Disruptions or problems are seen as episodic rather than systematic and are, as a result, dealt with by examining the personalities or characteristics of the offending individuals. By definition the "flaw" cannot be in the system, so the problem must be resolved by adjusting individual motivaton. So while Parsons may not himself have been a disengagement theorist, clearly disengagement theory was Parsonian in its functionalism.

This perspective of functionalist theory in general, and of the theory of disengagement in particular, explains the emphasis of Cumming's (1963) adjustment of the original theoretical statement. In attempting to account for the variety of styles and rates of disengagement, Cumming identified "some characteristics of aging people that might make an important difference to their patterns of disengagement" (1963: 378). Expressing a similar tendency to look to the individual for sources of varieties of disengagement, Henry (1964) attributed engagement and disengagement to the personality of the individual rather than to any social-systematic conditions. This suggestion by Henry contributed to the tendency to look to the individual for the answers to the problems raised by disengagement.

Under what circumstances might disengagement theory have seen varying rates and styles of disengagement as reflections of the unwillingness of old people to disengage because it is neither fulfilling nor beneficial for the individual? To incorporate this understanding, disengagement theory would have to accept the fact that one system may require for its equilibrium a circumstance that is dysfunctional for the equilibrium of another system. That is, while disengagement may be functional for the equilibrium of one social system such as the economic structure, it may be disruptive to the disengaging individual.

This idea illustrates the nature of Robert Merton's (1949) concept of dysfunction, " . . . those observed consequences which lessen the adaptation or adjustment of the system" (1949: 105). Merton saw the many structures of the human social order in complex interrelationship with one another. The consequences of actions or ideas might influence one system in a positive or system-maintaining way (functional) while detracting from the equilibrium of another (dysfunctional). If a master analysis of all the consequences of a given action, object, or idea could be conducted, the combination of its functions and dysfunctions for all systems involved could be calculated. The result, what Merton called "the net balance of the aggregate of consequences" (1949: 105) would reflect the extent to which a given action contributes to the systems it influences. Those actions, ideas, or objects which have a positive net aggregate of consequences are presumed to persist, while those which are negative in balance will be extinguished. Thus, while poverty may be obviously dysfunctional for one group of people, the poor, it may be functional for another more powerful group. Herbert Gans has predicted that to the extent that the net aggregate of consequences of poverty is positive, it will persist (Gans, 1972).

Similarly, disengagement may be wholly dysfunctional for disengaging individuals, the aged, but functional for other structures in society, such as the occupational order. If this is the case, then many of the problems associated with aging are inherent in the structure of society, a structure that depends for its equilibrium on the ability to disengage individuals at a manipulated rate. A Mertonian functionalism, informed by the concept of dysfunction, could have accounted for the system-based causes of disruptive disengagement. Disengagement theory as it was stated by Cumming and Henry, and as it was applied by later advocates, could not. In ignoring the dysfunctions of disengagement for individuals, disengagement theory has gone so far as to suggest that disengagement is actually functional or beneficial for the aged. This approach has allowed the reluctance to disengage to be attributed to variations in personality or in temperament of the disengaging individual rather than to its dysfunctions for the individual.

The Functions of Disengagement

Let us look at a possible listing of the functions of disengagement, including its consequences for a variety of systems (see Table 1).

In analyzing the material presented in Table 1, it must be recognized that a net aggregate of consequences does not necessarily reflect either the number of positive versus negative consequences listed or even the number of persons or systems for whom there are positive consequences versus the number for whom there are negative consequences. Each of these considerations must be further balanced by the relative power of the systems influenced in calculating the ultimate balance. Thus, if relatively few people who are very powerful in a

Table 1. Disengagement

Functional (contributes to the equilibrium of a system)	*Dysfunctional (detracts from the equilibrium of a system)*
For Social Structures:	For Social Structures:
1) Disengagement makes room for the young to occupy positions in the occupational structure, political structure, status hierarchy, and so on.	1) Disengagement means the loss of the talent, energy, and expertise of those who disengage.
2) Disengagement creates jobs in a variety of industries that serve the aged such as social services, medicine, retirement-home industry, leisure, and cosmetics.	2) Care for those who are disengaged drains the resources of the rest of society: for retirement benefits (Social Security); time spent on problems of the aged; health; poverty-related problems (Medicaid).
3) Disengagement creates a negative comparison group that allows the middle-aged to feel younger. This reinforces the norm of youthfulness.	3) Disengagement creates feelings of guilt in the rest of the population for "kicking the old out."
4) Disengagement (as retirement) provides a model for the rewards of working for many years, thus reinforcing the work ethic ("Pot of gold at the end of the rainbow").	For the Individual:
5) Disengagement provides work for social gerontologists.	4) Disengagement may contribute to poor health, poverty, loneliness, and poor self-image (especially when involuntary).
For the Individual:	
6) For those who want to disengage, disengagement allows withdrawal from unwanted societal attachments.	

society derive positive consequences for the systems they belong to from the existence of some behavior, but a relatively large number of powerless people are negatively affected by the same behavior, the net aggregate of consequences for that behavior would still be positive. That behavior would persist.

Activity Theory

As stated earlier, disengagement theory developed out of what its authors saw as an implicit (and false) assumption by previous researchers that successful aging was a matter of remaining as active and as involved as one had been in middle age. However, this idea has not been discarded and has been restated more recently as activity theory (Lemon, Bengtson, and Peterson, 1972) and so the debate with disengagement theory goes on. Disengagement theory claims that disengagement and role loss are functional for the individual, allowing the individual to develop a satisfying new equilibrium late in life. By contrast, activity theory suggests that there is a positive relationship between activity and life-satisfaction and that the greater the role loss, the lower the life-satisfaction. Thus, those who wish to enjoy their last years of life should continue to live as they had during their middle years right to the time death or illness stops them.

Like disengagement theory, activity theory is not *inherently* a victim-blaming approach. However, like disengagement theory, it has come to be interpreted and used as such. The belief that activity is associated with life-satisfaction in no way speaks to the issue of how inactivity among the aged comes about. Clearly, if activity theory had focused on the way social forces (such as mandatory retirement) *deny* the aged opportunities to remain active (especially to the extent that this occurs against their will) then activity theory could be nothing but a system-blaming approach. However, activity theory has been interpreted as another prescription for the aged to follow. They are implicitly criticized for their inactivity, and thus are blamed for their resulting decline. An example of this emphasis is evident in the following description of activity theory as an approach to "successful aging."

> The "activity" approach to successful aging holds that to age successfully *one* must maintain into old age the activity patterns and values typical of middle age. These values stress maintaining a large number of roles and being very active in them. To age successfully *the individual should avoid shrinkage of the life space and find substitute activities* when necessary.
>
> (Atchley, 1977: 219)

The maintenance of activity is the responsibility of the old person. By implication, inactivity must also be the responsibility of the elderly.

It should be recognized that the question of system-blaming versus victim-blaming leaves unresolved the issue of whether activity or disengagement is related to life satisfaction and for whom. What is at issue is that victim-blaming does not examine the role of social structures in creating the conditions under which the aged must exist.

Both disengagement and activity theories could have focused on either system forces or characteristics of the aged, but have strongly tended to do the latter. The same emphasis on characteristics of the aged, although to a lesser degree, appears in a third major theory of social aging.

Subculture Theory

In this approach Rose (1965b) suggests that the aged share a number of common interests and concerns and are forced by exclusion from interaction with other groups to interact primarily with one another. As a result, they have developed a subculture of the aged.[3] This subculture, a group whose beliefs and values are distinct from those of the larger society, is described by Rose as displaying a growing group-consciousness, pride, and self-esteem as shown in their "resentment at 'the way elderly people are being mistreated,' and indications of their taking social action to remove the sources of that resentment" (1965b: 15). Rose does not stress how the values, beliefs, and lifestyle of the aged differ from those of the rest of society. To do so would be to imply that the important factor in the social decline of the aged is their deviant set of values. Instead, the emphasis here is on how social forces isolate the aged and deny them access to the normal society. This is especially visible in Rosow's (1974) analysis of major institutional forces that have been brought to bear on the aged in American society. According to Rosow, these social forces have denied or diminished the position of the aged in many ways (see Table 2).

According to Rosow, as a result of these social forces the aged are devalued, stereotyped, excluded from society, experience role loss

---

[3]The concept of the aged as a subculture also appears as part of the theory of age stratification (Riley, 1971). Riley suggests that groups of people who are born during a given period of history share common experiences as they grow. As a result, they develop distinctive subcultures and society becomes stratified by age in much the same way it is stratified by social class.

Table 2.   How Social Forces Determine the Status of the Elderly

Institutional Factors for Aged	*Social-Structural Causes*
1) Property Ownership	Diffusion of ownership, separation between ownership and management, and increased opportunities for the young diminish control of aged over property.
2) Strategic Knowledge	Changes and increased rate of changes in technology and automation, evade the knowledge, skills, and esteem in which the elderly are held by the rest of society, reducing their authority.
3) Productivity	Technology has eliminated labor shortages and made older workers' marginal (or outdated) skills unnecessary.
4) Mutual Dependence	High productivity, economic growth and building, and some forms of government aid such as small business loans have increased personal independence and autonomy—this lessens need to get help from one's family.
5) Tradition and Religion	Our emphases on the secular and material reduce our need to see the elderly as a link to a symbolic and meaningful past. We are present oriented.
6) Kinship and Family	Occupational structure of society emphasizing mobility is best suited by nuclear family and so extended family with its concern for needs of aged declines.
7) Community Life	Specialization of roles (as in labor), residential mobility, and impersonal urban relationships weaken communities that once helped integrate the aged into society.

and role ambiguity. In order to avoid the painful identification with old age, Rosow suggests that the old often misidentify themselves as younger.

Subculture Theory and Victim-Blaming

Despite this strong emphasis on social-structural forces, however, subculture theory has also been used to blame the aged. Much of the literature in social gerontology expresses a view of the elderly as a subculture. This view of the subculture of the aged depicts their shared meanings and values as leading to their isolation from the rest of society, dependence on others for essential aid, feelings of inevitable decline, present time orientation, and so on. Those characteristics attributed to the aged by the rest of society such as lack of mobility, lowered levels of intelligence, strength, memory, and so on, increased rigidity and conservatism, and general uselessness contribute to the view that the aged are a subculture. The literature in gerontology has conceived of the elderly as a subculture whose meanings and values focus more on adaptation to their physiological, psychological, and sociological situations than on mobilization to change those situations.

In his analysis of how victim-blaming is applied to the poor in America, Ryan notes the use of the concept of "the culture of poverty" (Ryan, 1971). The poor have been described as differing from the rest of the society in the values that guide their lives (Lewis, 1966). Typically, the culture of the poor is described as being based on immediate gratification and little else. Their values are generally characterized by lacks: the lack of respect for education, the lack of a work ethic, the lack of concern for family solidarity, the lack of middle-class values. It is this set of "lacks" that comprises the culture of poverty, and to which continued poverty is attributed. Victim-blamers believe that if only these lacks can be eliminated by some sort of remedial programs the poor might pull out of their difficulties. This was not the emphasis Rose gave to subcultural theory in his original statement of the position in 1965. He seemed to be much more interested in the conditions that led to the development of the subculture of the aged and in the prospects for political action on the part of the aged to change those conditions. However, without specifically identifying itself as following subcultural theory, much of the literature in social gerontology seems to have taken a subcultural view of the aged in a victim-blaming way. Such an approach describes the concern of the elderly with the limited time they have left to live, with immediate problems of mobility and daily survival, and with achievements and memories from the past. It is these values that are believed to determine the orientation of the elderly to the world around them, and that are felt to influence the style of life of the aged. Thus, the elderly are advised, "if only you didn't have such concerns about the end of your life, or could stop focusing on past glories so much, or could stop worrying so much about your daily comfort, you wouldn't have problems." In our efforts to deal with the problems of aging, the perspective of blaming the victim has helped shape our programs.

"Helping" the Aged

We explored in the Blaming the Victim section of this chapter Ryan's (1971) distinction between exceptionalist and universalistic approaches to the solution of social problems. To refamiliarize you with his views, exceptionalist programs treat the symptoms of a problem by educating, socializing, or otherwise changing the characteristics of an individual. The aim is to enable that person to survive in a hostile environment. A program that teaches poor families the advisability of reading all contracts carefully so as to avoid being cheated is exceptionalist. A hot lunch program for children is exceptionalist since it does not deal at all with the conditions that make the program necessary in the first place. Exceptionalism is an approach to the symptoms, and is therefore specifically targeted to the sufferers. We can identify two exceptionalist approaches. The first is aimed at correcting the characteristics of the victims of a social problem—characteristics presumed to contribute to their difficulties. The second is designed to help victims of social problems to live with their problems, and in extreme cases, to survive them.

Universalistic programs deal with the social structures that cause problems and their symptoms, and are therefore much broader and, in the short run, much more expensive. Legislation against contracts that cheat consumers or take unfair advantage of them through subtle and difficult to understand conditions is universalistic. Such a universalistic approach not only focuses on the structure of the situation that contributes to a problem, but questions the very legal structure and supporting values that operate at the center of our legal order. Rather than attempting to educate the buyer to beware, it makes it illegal to cheat the buyer.

As with the poor and other people in society who are victims of our social problems, the aged have been the targets of numerous well-intentioned programs. It should be no surprise that given the types of theories and research that dominate gerontology, such programs have been exceptionalist rather than universalistic. The bulk of the programs designed to aid the aged are essentially survival aids. For those who are disabled by physical, psychological, or social trauma, access to housing, food, medical aid, transportation, and human companionship is provided in small expensive-to-administer doses. While one aged person who is depressed is sent to a psychologist, another may need funds to have new dentures fitted or glasses made. A program called meals on wheels brings hot food to isolated elderly at their homes or apartments. The nursing home or hospital for chronically ill aged is made available as last-resort housing. These are measures taken to help the aged survive. They are measures provided for a wholly dependent population who, without such services, would suffer either immeasurably greater deprivations or would die. The provision of these services for dependent populations has become extremely expensive for the society to support.

Many of these programs deal with the symptoms of old age. They do not deal with the social causes of the problem, but rather attempt to ameliorate the conditions of deprivation that result from them. They try to keep the old person alive and in minimal distress. However, there are also programs for the aged that try to correct their "defective" characters. For example, one service for the aged offers income counseling that teaches how to get the maximum use from a diminished income. People who have been used to living well on their earned incomes are taught how expensive it is to buy small quantities of food, since larger food containers cost less per unit amount. They learn that buying on time can be quite costly; they are told how to find inexpensive private housing or low income public housing, and how to budget from one social security or assistance check to the next. The implication of this type of program is that if the aged knew how to live on small amounts of money, if they had the benefit of being thrifty and careful with money (rather than extravagant and wasteful), they would have fewer problems. It is as though poverty were the fault of the aged poor rather than of the social system that has legalized mandatory retirement and otherwise created conditions contributing to financial loss and dependence. Teaching thrift to the elderly is a classical example of an exceptionalist program. The universalistic approach would require eliminating the economic and social conditions that cause individuals to be removed from their jobs at a given age, thereby becoming dependent upon others for economic aid. This approach would acknowledge that the poverty of the elderly is rooted in the structure of the occupational system rather than in the inability of the elderly to manage their money properly.

Another example of exceptionalist programs for the aged is the broad range of "keeping busy" activities that are run by old age and retirement homes, by entire communities for retirees, and by agencies that serve the elderly in a mixed-aged community. Volunteer work by the aged and arts and crafts programs (or diversional therapy shops— to borrow an instructive phrase from one rehabilitation center for the aged) are aimed at keeping the aged active—to combat feelings of isolation and uselessness among the elderly. However, the implication of these programs is that the aged tend toward inactivity and must be led to situations in which they can learn to be involved and active. This assumption is evident in the statement of a director of an older adults program who was discussing the needs of the elderly in a community.

> One of the objectives of the agency is to provide group and recreational programs for older people based on the assumption that the forced and self-imposed isolation of an individual from social contact with his peers and the community at large has a deteriorating effect. It is further believed that there should be opportunities for the restoration of older people through participation in group services which would re-engage them with their social environment and from which they would derive pleasure and satisfaction according to their interests, capacity and life styles.
>
> (Allen, 1966: 92)

These programs are aimed at changing in the elderly the tendency to become disengaged, as if that tendency were a characteristic that develops with age!

Another example of an exceptionalist program that combines the "retraining" and "keep busy" approaches is the retirement reorientation used to ease the transition to nonutilitarian or less utilitarian retirement roles (Bynum, Cooper, and Acuff, 1978). To the extent that such training socializes the aging to new roles, the characteristics of the aged are the target. To the extent that new activities being prepared for—such as volunteer work (sometimes called unpaid second careers) or focused leisure activities (such as crafts)—keeping the aged busy is the aim.

Similar to this type of program is the research on "interpersonal skill training" for institutionalized elderly (Berger and Rose, 1977). The researchers suggest that aged patients in institutions need to learn new social skills necessary for day-to-day interaction with others. "The patient must adjust to a range of new situations for which he may be unprepared" (Berger and Rose, 1977: 346). Also there is the report of a procedure called reality orientation, a "therapeutic approach attempted to help institutionalized residents who exhibit behaviors considered confused or disoriented in respect to spatio-temporal aspects of their lives'' (Citrin and Dixon, 1977: 39). In both cases the emphasis is on the way the aged must adjust to their new situation, whether it be institutionalization or merely disengagement of a milder sort. One must be retrained for this. Where is the emphasis on the structural, the social, conditions that compel such institutionalization and disengagement?

Why We Blame the Aged

Like other exceptionalist, victim-blaming approaches to social problems, programs to aid the elderly can be called successful only in a narrow sense. They prevent some people from dying from their poverty, illness, or loneliness, and they reduce the level of suffering of some others. To this extent they are vital. They are outright failures, however, in the effort to keep new generations of aging individuals from suffering the same losses as those before them. These programs are limited holding actions. Why do we pursue them? Why not spend the time, money, and effort to attack the roots of the problems? Were we to do so, in the long run, far fewer elderly would be dependent on expensive caretaking programs and the costs to them and to society would be greatly diminished.

That we do not attack the roots of the problem involves the tendency to believe in the particular variety of order and stability that forms our existing social structures and institutions. We express our faith in these structures by placing the blame for disruptions to order on external forces. *We would rather believe that problems in society are external, deviant, exceptional, even random, so that the essential correctness of our social order may be affirmed.* For example, it is an expression of belief in our social order to suggest that criminal behavior is the result of characteristics of the criminal rather than some facet of the legal or political system to which we belong, or to attribute the poverty of an individual to his or her characteristic lack of motivation or skills rather than to the inability of the educational or occupational structure to provide opportunities for wealth. Blaming the victim is an outgrowth of that conservatism which cannot find fault with things as they are.

Ryan distinguishes between blaming the victim and '' . . . old fashioned conservative ideologies.'' The latter simply dismiss victims as inferior, genetically defective, or morally unfit; the emphasis is on the intrinsic, even hereditary, defect. The former shifts its emphasis to the environmental causation (Ryan, 1971). Ryan notes that this approach permits liberals to protect their belief in the essential stability of the social structure and to blame the victims of social problems anyway. They can claim that the debilitating defect of the individual is not inherited but acquired, such as through faulty socialization. As a result the liberal can call for rehabilitative programs that contribute to feelings of good will toward the poor, and at the same time ignore the social forces that create the problem.

It is most important that the contribution of the social structure to the existence of these problems be ignored by conservative and liberal alike since each benefits from the existence of that structure. Changes in the broader structure that would eliminate or reduce the problems of society might also reduce or eliminate the advantaged positions of those who are powerful enough to affect policy. Simple self-interest motivates victim-blamers. While conservatives may feel no guilt about blaming the victim for his "natural" inferiority, liberals have found a way to avoid guilt, and even to feel humanitarian about the programs they advocate to help the victim with his or her "acquired" problem.

The victims of social problems are usually members of minority groups. They are separated from the advantaged members of society by physical and social distance, and often by physical and cultural differences. The literature of intergroup relations has suggested that these differences and the perceived distance between majority and minority group members make it easier for the dominant group to direct prejudice and discrimination against the subordinate group (Allport, 1954).

A difficulty arises when the people who are blamed are either similar to, or closely involved in, the social networks of the actual victim-blamers. Thus, blaming the aged has consequences for the feelings of self-worth of those younger people who have aged parents, friends and relatives, and who recognize that they will also be old one day themselves. The anxiety we feel about growing old, the feelings of guilt that arise from institutionalizing one's own parents, the tendency to distinguish between one's own aged family members and other old people as "not the same thing," the fact that gerontology has only recently become an issue for study—all attest to the problem of facing up to the deprivations of a group of people so intimately connected with ourselves.

We blame the aged because, given the present structure of the occupational and political and social orders, it is convenient to do so. It enables us to maintain that structure by disengaging the aged to the detriment of many. We justify that action by considering the aged a special group of people for whom separation from social involvement is beneficial or at least just due. The difficulties associated with this process are attributed to the unfortunate characteristics that we presume the aged to acquire with the years. We ignore the problem (though it may seem inevitable given our existing social structure) or fatalistically attribute all of it to an impersonal biological fate. In any case we have not, until recently, even begun to recognize the possibility that the difficulties of growing old may be as much the result of social as of biological forces. Clearly, old age is partly a biological phenomenon. However, poverty, isolation, and feelings of uselessness are not. If there is a large component of social force in the problems of aging, then it is most appropriate that a theory that does not blame the aged should come from social gerontology.

The Problem of the Young

Our discussion of how theories of social gerontology have blamed the aged, or have tended to be interpreted in that way, has suggested that each theory had within it the potential for a different approach to this problem. Disengagement theory might have exposed how the structures of society benefit from the predictable withdrawal of its members at a given age. Subcultural theory might have studied why the aged are treated in a way differently from the rest of society, or focused on the conflict between the society and the aged over the treatment they have received. Activity theory might have led to an analysis of the ways opportunities for activity are denied the aged by the structures of society and by negative attitudes toward the aged. As we have seen, however, these theories have focused on characteristics of the aged almost to the exclusion of attention to the way social forces have contributed to the problems of the aged, even though the potential for a different approach has existed since the beginnings of social gerontology. Had the underlying social causes been examined, we might well have seen the problem of the aged rechristened the problem of the young.

As shown earlier in this chapter, the behaviors and social conditions that we choose to label as problems can change over time. For example, discussion of sex-role conflicts has only recently been included in many social problems courses. Also, how we name a problem reveals our assumptions about it and serves some underlying interests. William Ryan, showing how this process applies to victim blaming, writes, "We have been comfortable for years with the 'Negro problem,' a term that clearly implies that the existence of Negroes is somehow a problematic fact. *Ebony* magazine turned the tables recently and renamed the phenomenon as 'the white problem in America,' which may be a good deal more accurate" (1971: 12). In its most extreme form, this labeling process is reminiscent of the political purposes of the Nazis in identifying "the Jewish problem."

The problems the aged suffer in American society have long been called problems of aging or of the aged. But to the extent that these difficulties are the result of treatment by the rest of society, the problem is misnamed. According to Irving Rosow, the problem is really a problem of the young: "The crucial people in the aging problem are not the old, but the younger age groups, for it is the rest of us who determine the status and position of the old person in the social order" (Rosow, 1962: 191). Misnaming the problem allows and compels us to focus our energies in limited ways. We study the old and consequently aim all our resources at ameliorative programs for them. In the absence of theories that hold some facet of the social structure other than the aged themselves responsible for the difficulties of aging, how can we be expected to develop policies to deal with the source of the problem rather than with its symptoms?

Rosow contends that to solve this problem we need "a basic reordering of our national aspirations and values, of which the aging problem is but a token. Anything less than this will see us concentrating only on superficial symptoms, especially tangible ones like housing the aged, and nibbling at the tattered edges of our problems without penetrating to their heart" (1962: 191).

In order to develop an approach to this problem that does not deal solely with the characteristics of the aged, it is necessary to consider the attitude of the rest of society toward the aged and toward the process of aging. Are there some ideas about aging that are characteristic of the entire culture? What is the place of the elderly in the structure of society? Are there some principles of group relations that might explain the treatment the aged receive from the younger members of society?

Elements of already existing theories and a number of newer ideas seem to be suggesting a system-blaming approach. The age stratification view (Riley, 1976) has been particularly concerned with aging as an element of the larger social structure of a society. This is especially apparent in its discussion of the relationships (such as segregation and conflict) between various age strata. Activity theory and re-engagement (Jacobs and Vinick, 1977) have suggested the efficacy of not treating the aged as a special group distinguishable from the middle-aged. A number of researchers have suggested that the aged have suffered age discrimination (Rosen and Jerdee, 1976) and prejudice (Tuckman and Lorge, 1953a; Harris, 1975).

In searching for a perspective that would focus on the social forces that contribute to the problems of the aged, it has become apparent that the aged have been treated as a group by the rest of society. Laws permitting mandatory retirement and providing inadequate incomes among those who had been stable, successful wage earners through their middle years have contributed to this second-class treatment of the aged. Similarly, the existence of negative stereotypes about the aged as a group have led to the conclusion that the aged in American society constitute a disadvantaged minority group that lacks the power to determine its own social fate.

Summary

Chapter Two has presented an evaluation of the research and theories in gerontology. Much of this work is found to take the perspective of blaming the victim (Ryan, 1971).

Blaming the victim attributes some social problem to the characteristics of the victims of that problem. This allows one to focus efforts to deal with the problem on changing the characteristics of the victim (exceptionalist approach) rather than on the social conditions that created the problem (universalist approach). Thus, victim-blaming allows one to maintain a belief in the essential stability of a social system, attributing problems to extrasystemic causes.

As Ryan notes the literature of gerontology has blamed the aged in much the same way that we have blamed the poor for their condition. The research in the physiology and psychology of aging has, by choosing to focus on characteristics of the aged, contributed to this tendency. Similarly, the theories and findings of social gerontology have tended to blame the aged.

Disengagement theory has tended to focus on the way individuals disengage from societal roles rather than on the conditions in society that make disengagement necessary. Role theory has concentrated on characteristics of aged individuals as they adapt to the role of the old person, rather than on the type of social order that maintains such roles. Subculture theory has viewed the values of the aged as contributing to their isolation rather than on the reasons such values develop. Activity theory has emphasized the responsibility of the aged to remain active and involved rather than the social forces that have denied them opportunities for valued activity.

Given the prevalence of victim-blaming in social gerontology, most strongly through disengagement theory, a non-victim-blaming approach to the problems of aging seems called for.

Chapter Three

The Aged as a Minority Group

Concept of Minority Group

The concept of minority group has provided a valuable frame of reference for understanding the experiences of groups of people who, as Wirth (1945: 347) long ago observed, "because of physical or cultural characteristics, are singled out from the others in the society in which they live for differential and unequal treatment." For decades, the use of the minority concept centered largely on the problems encountered by racial, ethnic, and religious groups such as blacks, Jews, or Mexican-Americans, whose members have served as the targets of prejudice and discrimination. More recently, the minority concept has also been applied to women, homosexuals, and the physically disabled (Sagarin, 1971; Davis, 1978).

Minority group is an orienting concept. In contrast to victim-blaming explanations of inequality, the minority group concept alerts us, first of all, to the fact that individuals are frequently assigned a subordinate position in a society by virtue of some ascribed characteristic—a characteristic over which they have little or no control. Thus, the minority concept directs our attention to the *treatment*—individual as well as institutional—of the members of one group by the members of another group. In race relations, for example, the application of the minority concept has led investigators to recognize that the problem of race in American society is at least in part a "white problem." That is, in order to understand the subordinate status of black Americans, we must first understand the way prejudice and discrimination are directed against black America by white America.

We intend to show that the minority group concept can be applied as well to the experiences of the elderly in America. They have been victims of prejudice and discrimination and have responded collectively in ways that are predictable based on their status as a minority.[1]

Streib's "Are the Aged a Minority Group?"

One convenient way to begin this discussion is to confront directly gerontologist Gordon Streib's (1965) influential and frequently cited article, "Are the Aged a Minority Group?" In it he concludes that the elderly are not a minority group and that the minority perspective only obscures our understanding of the experiences of old people in American society.[2]

According to Streib, the aged are not a minority group because they fail to meet the criteria suggested by Wirth's definition. Streib argues that the aged do not constitute a group in any sociological sense, are not stereotyped in a negative manner, and are not discriminated against based on age. What is more, Streib arbitrarily adds to his criteria that the minority status *must* cover the entire life cycle of an individual. This would, of course, exclude the elderly since their minority status does not begin until late in life.

The Minority Concept as an Ideal Type

In a sense, Streib is correct when he argues that the criteria for minority status are not completely satisfied in the case of the elderly in America. What he fails to recognize is that *no group of people,* including those we typically identify as minorities, *totally fits the definition.* The minority group concept is an ideal type; an exaggeration or caricature of reality that is useful for comparative purposes precisely because it does not totally describe the experiences of any group of people

---

[1]Others have proposed applying the minority concept to the aged. See, for example, Barron (1953), Breen (1960), Davis (1978), Palmore and Whittington (1971), Rose and Peterson (1965), and Rosow (1962).

[2]We agree with Streib that the size of a group does not necessarily indicate whether or not its members hold minority status in a society. Numerical strength alone has little to do with the ability of a group to exercise power or maintain prestige. Small groups have been known to possess excessive power and wealth; very large groups have been severely oppressed.

(Weber, 1947). Thus, minority groups are different from one another with respect to a number of important characteristics including whether or not minority membership covers the entire life cycle, degree and kind of group consciousness, and degree and kind of discrimination.

Negative Group Consciousness

Consider Streib's contention that the elderly fail to constitute a group in any sociological sense. As recently as 1976, Streib repeated his argument that "the aged do not identify with their age mates, and they tend to have a low feeling of group consciousness" (1976: 169). In making this statement, Streib ignores an important aspect of minority group consciousness: it frequently takes a negative form, including ambivalence and self-hatred. Many individuals seek either actively or passively to disassociate themselves from their minority status; they prefer to avoid identification with their group (Lincoln, 1961).

To illustrate this concept, we might ask, "what is the origin of black subculture?" It is certainly not based on positive identification with the continent of Africa! First of all, there was tremendous cultural diversity among the African tribes involved in the New World slave trade. Black Africans were brought from many different places, representing a variety of languages, religions, and political structures (Elkins, 1959). Secondly, the significance of African heritage was shattered very quickly after the arrival of slaves in the New World. According to Frazier (1949), the organization of slave labor—in particular, its need for isolation and mobility—assured the destruction of the African family system. "Under such circumstances, African languages were lost and the African social organization could not be reconstituted in the new environment" (Frazier, 1949: 20–21).

Since their aboriginal culture and social organization were smashed, black Americans were forced to adjust to the new conditions and become culturally like the white Americans. Rather than common ethnic identity, it was to a great extent common suffering that united black Americans in a shared subculture and identity. As Lincoln suggests,

> The "nationalism" of the American Negro is not voluntary,
> prompted by a desire to set himself apart in order to preserve some
> cultural values. It is, rather, a defensive response to external
> forces—hostile forces which threaten his creative existence. It is a
> unity born of the wish not to conserve but to *escape* a set of conditions (1961: 45).

Since Clark and Clark (1958), studies of race consciousness have repeatedly found that many black children by the age of three or four already have developed negative group consciousness (or racial awareness). They frequently show clear-cut preferences for white rather than black dolls and even misidentify themselves as white (Greenwald and Oppenheim, 1968; Morland, 1972).

Unfortunately, negative group consciousness does not end with adulthood. Black adults have been found to accept negative stereotypes regarding blacks (Simpson and Yinger, 1972) and to value lighter skin color (Seeman, 1956). It has been estimated that as many as 50,000 very light-skinned blacks annually "pass" into the white community in order to avoid the stigma of minority status (Berry and Tischler, 1978).

It is, of course, difficult to estimate precisely how many of the elderly attempt to "pass" for middle-aged. Clearly, however, many elders do not wish to be identified as "old," "elderly," or "aged" (Taves and Hansen, 1963)—indicating group consciousness of a negative kind. Hence, the consistent preference of a majority of the elderly to be called "senior citizens" (liked by 50 percent), "retired persons" (liked by 53 percent), and "mature Americans" (liked by 55 percent) (Harris, 1975).

Minority-group Hostility

In connection with his insistence on group consciousness as part of his definition of minority group, Streib (1976) also emphasizes the importance of hostility against the majority group as expressed by minority members. He states that "while membership organizations of senior citizens have grown greatly in the last decade, such groups have relatively low hostility towards out groups" (Streib, 1976: 169). In the extreme, the more militant Gray Panthers involve only a minute percentage of older Americans.

Streib's insistence that minority groups must express hostility toward majority group members may stem in part from his absolute version of the minority concept and his misreading of the experiences of racial and ethnic minorities. For example, though they had been oppressed for some 350 years, black Americans did not engage in massive demonstrations and protests until the 1960s (Pettigrew, 1971). Moreover, even during this relatively violent period of history, only a tiny fraction of the black population expressed their approval of such groups as the Black Muslims or of Elijah Muhammad. By contrast, the overwhelming majority disapproved of "Black Nationalism" and in-

dicated they would not riot as a means of protest. Only 11 percent sa.
that blacks "should give up working together with whites and just
depend on their own people" (Brink and Harris, 1966: 67). The majority reported a preference for racial integration at work, in neighbor-
hoods, and at school.

As we will show in Chapters Four and Five, the elderly too
have begun to protest and demonstrate in an effective manner and to
emerge as a cohesive political force as well. Bengtson and Cutler's
recent analysis of age consciousness among the elderly suggests the
possibility of a sequence of events not unlike that associated with the
rise of race consciousness among black Americans:

> . . . As a greater proportion of the population is included in the older
> age categories, as future generations of old people have the educa-
> tional resources and political experience to actively participate in
> political controversies concerning issues of social and financial alloca-
> tion, and as age consciousness and subjective age identification
> among the elderly increase—under these circumstances generational
> analysis predicts the emergence of generation units among the elderly.
> And while not all old people will evidence age consciousness, those
> who do become the focus of generation units potentially represent a
> significant force for social and political change (1976: 156).

The "Entire Life Cycle" Criterion

As indicated earlier, Streib argues that the minority status
must cover the entire life cycle of an individual. What he fails to recognize is that application of this criterion excludes numerous individuals
not "born into" a minority group, who subsequently convert (for
example, Christians who adopt Judaism or heterosexuals who embrace
homosexuality). His criterion also excludes millions of newcomers to
America—immigrants from Europe who did not become members of a
minority until arriving in the New World.

Streib may have meant to argue that minority-group status
must have the *potential* to cover the entire life cycle of an individual.
Application of this version of his criterion would exclude the elderly,
while including religious converts as well as immigrants. It should be
emphasized, however, that Streib's criterion (even in this modified
form) is an arbitrarily imposed standard not found in sociological definitions of minority groups, including Wirth's. It makes as much sense to
insist that the minority status be associated exclusively with the entire
life cycle as it does to insist that it be limited to dark-skinned peoples (as
some black Americans may prefer to do) or to immigrants alone.

ib's (1965) Criteria for Establishing Minority-Group
as Applied to the Elderly in American Society

	Situation of Elders:
ot the group possess identifying characteristics throughout the life cycle?	No. Obviously, old age does not begin until late in life. However, this criterion is not recognized by others in the field of majority-minority relations. It arbitrarily excludes many groups traditionally regarded as having minority status by experts in the field of ethnic and race relations.
2) Does the majority group hold stereotypes about the aged?	Yes. Surveys conducted during the 1950s, 1960s, and 1970s, as well as studies of popular humor, have uncovered negative stereotypes regarding characteristics of the elderly.
3) Do the aged possess a sense of group identity?	Yes. Studies have indicated very intense negative group consciousness. Just as in the case of other minorities (for example, blacks), many elders attempt to "pass" for majority group members and deny their minority status. What is more, there are no absolute criteria for identifying elders just as there are none automatically to identify blacks. Such definitions vary by time and place.
4) Is there readiness to organize as a political pressure group?	The aged have begun to protest and demonstrate. Their membership organizations, which have grown steadily during the last decade, have effectively agitated for favorable legislation such as Medicare and increased age of mandatory retirement. Just as in the case of other minorities, groups of elders tend to express relatively low levels of hostility toward outgroups.
5) Do the aged have differential access to power, privilege, and rights?	Until recently, the Age Discrimination in Employment Act did not apply to individuals over 65. The recent increase in mandatory retirement to age 70, though benefiting many persons in their sixties, continues to discriminate against numerous elders. Few, if any, other minority groups in our society have been denied employment to this extent.
6) Are the aged victims of deprivation?	Yes. One-quarter to one-third of the population aged 65 and older have incomes below the poverty level. Their housing tends to be of poor quality and their access to needed services and facilities is limited.

There is absolutely nothing in the sociological meaning of the minority concept that compels us to exclude the elderly merely because they have not *always* been elderly!

Sociological Focus of Minority-Group Concept

The concept of minority group has a distinctly sociological focus. It informs us that group membership is frequently determined by the definitions that *society* chooses to impose upon individuals, regardless of their actual physical characteristics or their personal preferences.

For example, when we ask, "Who is black?" the most obvious answer makes reference to physical characteristics such as dark skin, coarse hair, broad nose, and so on. Yet definitions of blackness have varied widely by place and time. There simply are no absolute criteria for racial identification. In the United States, although laws regarding race identity have varied from state to state, anyone found to possess even a trace of black ancestry (or Negro blood) is for most purposes regarded as black. Thus, a light-skinned, fair-haired, blue-eyed American who is discovered to have a single—even distant—ancestor of African descent is likely to be classified as belonging to the black race. No such racial distinctions are automatically imposed in Latin American countries such as Puerto Rico or Brazil, where individuals who are not obviously black are regarded as mulatto or white. Also in contrast to American definitions of race, South Africa has traditionally regarded individuals of mixed racial ancestry as a legally and socially distinct group, whose members enjoy fewer privileges than whites but more privileges than blacks (Berry and Tischler, 1978).

Not unlike the situation of race, old age is as much a product of social definition as of biology. Who is old? Is it necessarily and exclusively the individual who has gray hair and wrinkled skin? Like the varying physical characteristics that differentiate members of the same racial group from one another, physical differences between individuals of the same age make group identification on such a basis problematic, if not impossible. A person is old in our society when he or she is defined as such by the dominant forces in society. More specifically, an old person is one who is forced to retire, who must show an identification card to secure his senior citizen discount, and who receives Old Age Survivor's Insurance (Social Security) and pensions, upon reaching a certain age.

To be old in America is typically to live on a fixed income at a substantially reduced level; to compete for housing; to have limited access to needed services, facilities, family, friends, and self-enrichment opportunities (Carp, 1976).

Thus, in our society, old age begins at 65 or 70. This is the criterion usually employed for administrative purposes relating to eligibility for retirement, pensions, social security, insurance, and housing; it has been given official sanction by the federal government. In other societies, however, old age (as indicated by old-age benefits, retirement, or other changes in role expectation) is defined as beginning as early as 40 or 50. This is true, for example, among the Igbo of Eastern Nigeria and in the Samoan Islands of Polynesia (Cowgill and Holmes, 1972; Cain, 1976; Schulz, 1976).

The sociological meaning of the aged status is not universally associated with chronological age. In preliterate societies, chronological age is frequently viewed as unimportant, if known at all. Instead, old age is marked by relative age; that is, by changes in the roles that individuals are expected to play, for example, by the death of a father or older brother, by the role of extended family head, by the grandparent role, or by the age at which the role of elder is achieved (Cowgill and Holmes, 1972).

Finally, whereas legal codes in many societies have distinguished between children and adults, most between adults and elders have appeared during the twentieth century. As Cain (1976: 352) observes, "to a considerable extent, legal age issues have become bimodal, that is, age based laws focus upon either the withholding of adult status from the minor or the withdrawal of adult status from the elderly."

Ageism as a Form of Prejudice and Discrimination

An important consequence of viewing a group as a minority is to raise the possibility that prejudice and discrimination are directed against its members. Prejudice is interpersonal hostility but of a special kind: it is directed against individuals *based on their membership in a minority group* (Levin, 1975). This indicates that there are other kinds of hostility that may have nothing to do with prejudice. For example, two individuals—one young, the other old—may not get along because they disagree about basic values or because their personalities clash. Such hostility between them is not prejudice—it may be unrelated to their group memberships. They simply do not like one another as individuals.

In sharp contrast, a young person who believes that the aged are rigid, meddlesome, and unproductive may direct his hostility against anyone over 65 based on the image in his head and not on actual behavior. In such a case, we can say that the younger person's hostility is based on the older person's group membership; that is, the younger is prejudiced against the elderly.

Certain forms of prejudice and discrimination are so pervasive that they deserve a separate term. For example, prejudice against blacks is frequently known as racism; prejudice against women is commonly referred to as sexism. In 1969, Robert Butler coined the word "ageism" to refer to prejudice against old people.

Psychologically, ageism can be regarded as an *attitude*—a negative evaluation that serves to orient individuals toward old people as a group. In particular, ageism as an attitude frequently predisposes individuals to *discriminate;* that is, to avoid contact, victimize, or otherwise do injury to old people based on their age status alone (Levin, 1975). In American society, ageism has become more than a matter of individual attitude; it has become *institutionalized* in a number of legal and moral codes that are widely known and enforced. Institutionalized ageism can be clearly seen in mandatory retirement laws that have traditionally discriminated against Americans after the age of 65 (presently, after the age of 70), and in the widespread existence of substandard nursing homes.

But ageism is more than a tendency to discriminate. It also consists of "pictures in our heads" as Walter Lippman (1922) described them. It is the *stereotypes* or beliefs that we hold regarding the members of a category. Research has uncovered commonly accepted stereotypes about virtually every minority group in our society. The Irish are seen as "pugnacious," the Italians as "impulsive," the Chinese as "sly," the Turks as "cruel," the blacks as "lazy," and the Jews as "shrewd" (Katz and Braly, 1933). As we shall see, stereotypes are frequently employed in order to justify discrimination against minorities.

Images of the Aged

Butler has summarized the multitude of stereotypes associated with old age as follows:

> An older person thinks and moves slowly. He does not think as he used to or as creatively. He is bound to himself and can no longer

change or grow. He can learn neither well nor swiftly and, even if he could, he would not wish to. Tied to his personal traditions and growing conservatism, he dislikes innovations and is not disposed to new ideas. Not only can he not move forward, he often moves backward. He enters a second childhood, caught up in increasing egocentricity and demanding more from his environment than he is willing to give to it. Sometimes he becomes an intensification of himself, a caricature of a lifelong personality. He becomes irritable and cantankerous, yet shallow and enfeebled. He lives in his past; he is behind the times. He is aimless and wandering of mind, reminiscing and garrulous. Indeed, he is a study in decline, the picture of mental and physical failure. He has lost and cannot replace friends, spouse, job, status, power, influence, income. He is often stricken by diseases which, in turn, restrict his movement, his enjoyment of food, the pleasures of well-being. He has lost his desire and capacity for sex. His body shrinks, and so too does the flow of blood to his brain. His mind does not utilize oxygen and sugar at the same rate as formerly. Feeble, uninteresting, he awaits his death, a burden to society, to his family, and to himself (1975: 6).

Age stereotypes have been with us for a long time. Tuckman and Lorge (1953a) asked 147 graduate students in psychology to indicate their agreement or disagreement with a number of statements about old people. As shown in Table 4, they found substantial acceptance of stereotypes associated with the aged. Despite the fact that their subjects were well acquainted with psychology and had enrolled in a course involving the aging process, there was a high level—sometimes reaching 90 percent—of agreement that old people are set in their ways, are conservative, are bossy, and like to doze in a rocking chair.

More than a decade after the Tuckman and Lorge study, McTavish (1971) found that approximately three-fourths of a sample of 1469 American adults agreed that old people "are apt to complain" and "are sometimes inconsiderate of the views of younger persons." More than one-third of his sample felt that old people are "annoying."

Recent research indicates that stereotyping continues to be an integral part of public images of the aged. In 1975, the National Council on the Aging reported the results of a Harris (1975) survey of American adults that was conducted to determine popular images of aging. The results obtained by Harris were generally consistent with those obtained decades earlier. As shown in Table 5, American adults typically agreed that "most people over 65" were not very physically active, not very good at getting things done, not very useful members of their community, not very bright and alert, not very open-minded and adaptable, and not very sexually active.

Table 4. Percentage of Graduate Students Expressing Agreement
with Selected Statements from Tuckman and Lorge's (1953a)
Old People Questionnaire

Statement	% Agreement (N = 147)
They are set in their ways	90
They are old fashioned	68
They are conservative	90
They like to think about the good old days	87
They dislike any changes or interference with established ways of doing things	80
They walk slowly	87
They have poor coordination	66
They have lost most of their teeth	79
They usually live with their children	57
They like to give advice	85
They are bossy	67
They love life	81
They like to be waited on	51
They are lonely	61
They repeat themselves in conversation	61
They are forgetful	57
They like to doze in a rocking chair	57

Table 5. Characteristics Attributed to "Most People over 65" by
American Adults (Harris, 1975)

Characteristic:	% Agreement
Very warm and friendly	74
Very wise from experience	64
Very physically active	41
Very good at getting things done	35
Very bright and alert	29
Very useful members of their community	23
Very open-minded and adaptable	21
Very sexually active	5

On a lengthy list of characteristics generally attributed to individuals who are productive and effective, Harris found only two which most Americans were willing to associate with "most people over 65." The majority agreed that older people are very warm and friendly, and very wise from experience. The overall image of old Americans is far from flattering. As Harris (1975: 46) suggests, "seen as nice old folks who have benefited from the trials and tribulations of life, most people over 65 are not viewed, however, as very active, efficient or alert people."

More indirect approaches to the study of attitudes toward the elderly also indicate ageism. Palmore's (1971) content analysis of 264 popular jokes and humorous quotations about aging showed that the majority make negative references to aging and the aged. Among the most negative jokes were those dealing with appearance, declining physical and mental ability, old maids, and the desire to conceal old age. More recently, Richman (1977) compared 100 jokes about the aged with 160 jokes dealing with children. He found that 66 percent of the jokes about old age were negative toward the older person, whereas over 70 percent of the jokes about children were positive toward the child. Like Palmore before him, Richman uncovered negative themes concerning age concealment, loss of attractiveness, and physical and mental decline. In addition, he found a number of negative jokes about age as undesirable sui generis, sexual decline, death, and nonacceptance of age-related tasks.

Stereotypes and Discrimination

Stereotypes are used to justify discrimination. If old people are intellectually inferior and unproductive, they should be forced to retire. If they prefer disengagement, then they should be physically separated from the young. Job-related stereotypes about the aged are particularly damaging since they may frequently be used to justify firing older workers. In an early study, Tuckman and Lorge (1952b) investigated the extent to which 147 graduate students in psychology accepted some popularly held stereotypes regarding older workers. They found that as many as 74 percent of these students agreed that older workers look to the past, are slow, need longer rest periods more often, need more time to learn new operations, and are slow to catch new ideas.

More recently, Rosen and Jerdee (1976) studied the nature of job-related age stereotypes by asking 106 respondents—56 realtors and 50 undergraduate business students—to indicate the degree to which a number of characteristics described the average 60-year-old male and the average 30-year-old male. Only on ratings associated with job stability such as reliability and honesty was the older man favored. On characteristics associated with job performance capacity and potential for development, the 60-year-old person was rated consistently lower than the 30-year-old person. In particular, the younger man was seen as more productive, efficient, motivated, capable of working under pressure, innovative, creative, and logical. The older man was seen as more accident prone. The younger man was also perceived to be more ambitious, eager, future-time oriented, receptive to new ideas, capable of learning, adaptable, and versatile. The older man was perceived to be more rigid and dogmatic.

To determine the influence of these job-related age stereotypes on managerial decisions, Rosen and Jerdee (1976) asked 142 undergraduate business students to play the role of a division manager by making a series of decisions about the fate of an employee involved in an "on-the-job" incident. In each of six incidents, the employee's age was experimentally manipulated by specifying his age (for example, 61 years old versus 32 years old) or by describing him as a "younger" or an "older" employee. For example, to examine the influence of age on perceptions of untrainability, Rosen and Jerdee depicted as either 30 years old or 60 years old a computer programmer whose technical skills had become obsolete. Subjects were asked to decide whether to terminate the programmer or to retrain him. Results obtained by the investigators confirmed their hypothesis that stereotypes about physical and mental decline in older workers contribute to on-the-job discrimination against them. When the employee was described as an older person, subjects were significantly less likely to recommend that the company provide him with selection, promotion, and training opportunities. Instead, they were likely to suggest ignoring him or firing him as an appropriate managerial response.

A recent study indicates that the age of a lecturer may under certain conditions influence the willingness of students to attend his classroom. Levin and Levin (1977) asked 294 male undergraduates to read the resume of an industrial sociologist "who wishes to come to the campus to talk about consumer research." One-third of the students were told that he was 25 years old, one-third that he was 50, and one-third that he was 75. In addition, the income of the lecturer was varied by informing one-half of the students that he made $5900 annually and the other half that he made $59,000 annually. After reading the resume of the visiting lecturer, all students were asked to indicate how likely they would be to attend "a talk" and "an informal discussion and coffee hour" with the visiting lecturer.

Our results suggested that students' willingness to attend a talk was not influenced by the age of the lecturer—students were just as likely to attend whether the lecturer's age was 25, 50, or 75 years of age.[3] Attendance at the informal discussion and coffee hour was a

[3]A similar finding has been reported by Bell and Stanfield (1973).

different story, however. When the lecturer was identified as having low income, students were significantly less willing to attend when he was old rather than middle-aged or young. By contrast, age made no difference at all when the lecturer was identified as having high annual income.

What do these findings mean? They seem to indicate, first of all, that the expectation that social distance can be maintained from an old person may determine whether age becomes an important consideration in an individual's willingness to interact. In this study, age did not appear to influence the likelihood of attending a formal talk where social distance between teacher and student seems easy to maintain. By contrast, age was very much a factor in the willingness of students to attend an informal discussion and coffee hour where much greater social intimacy is implied. This interpretation is supported by previous research that suggests that college students are less willing to become personally involved (for example, as close friends) with elderly than with middle-aged or young persons (Golde and Kogan, 1959; Long, Ziller, and Thompson, 1960).

Another factor in the Levin and Levin (1977) study is the interaction between age and income of the lecturer. For the situation of an informal discussion and coffee hour, the lecturer's age became a determining factor only when the lecturer was also identified as poor. This seems to indicate that wealth can help overcome the social stigma of old age. But it should also be noted that poverty characterizes the life style of many aged Americans, and that prospects of widespread wealth for the aged are remote at best.

As with the treatment of other minority groups, stereotypes and discrimination are interdependent. Negative beliefs, feelings, and tendencies to act negatively toward the aged "justify" discrimination against them. The belief that older workers are slow or untrainable is used in the decision not to hire, not to promote, or even to fire them. To the extent that this takes place, opportunities for older people (and therefore examples of the inaccuracy of the stereotypes) become rare. This in turn reinforces the stereotypes. There is no need to identify a starting point in the cycle. Stereotypes about the aged and discrimination against them are mutually reinforcing, and so must both be examined.

Stereotypes—Myth and Reality

How much truth is there to the stereotypes usually associated with older people? Evidence obtained from numerous studies strongly suggests that images of the aged are based more on myth than reality, more on fiction than on fact.

Sexual Inactivity. To illustrate, let us examine widely accepted stereotypes about the "sexless older years." As you may recall from Table 5 only 5% of those surveyed agreed that old people are very sexually active. For the aged, sex is generally regarded as negligible or unimportant and older people suspected of having some interest in sex are frequently viewed as deviant if not lecherous (Rubin, 1968).

However, fact contradicts the stereotype. First of all, there is no automatic cutoff date at which old age begins and sexual desire ends (Rubin, 1968). A gradual weakening of sexual interest and activity frequently accompanies advancing age, especially among men. But the *rate* of sexual decline is no greater during the last few decades of life than it is during earlier decades (Kinsey, Pomeroy, and Martin, 1948; Masters and Johnson, 1966). And according to a survey of sexual activity by Newman and Nichols (1960), only individuals 75 years or older have significantly lower levels of sexual activity.

In a series of studies of 254 men and women aged 60 to 94, Pfeiffer, Verwoerdt, and Wang (1969) report finding significant patterns of declining, stable, as well as increasing sexual activity among older people. Additionally, the degree of sexual activity among older women was found to be strongly influenced by the availability of a male partner who was both socially acceptable and sexually capable. Death and impotence of their spouse were the most common reasons given by older women for the cessation of sexual intercourse.

Shere Hite's (1976) nationwide study of 3000 women, ages 14 to 78, indicates that many older women believe that their sexual pleasure increases with age. Following are typical responses of older women to the questions, "How does age affect sex? Does desire for sex increase or decrease, or neither, with age? Enjoyment of sex?"

> Sex definitely gets better as you get older. In the past two years, I have simply done as I damn well pleased when it came to sex. I live every day as if it were my last. It's great.
> I think that men are conned into believing that it decreases in age for them. I don't think it decreases drastically for anyone, *especially* for women. My best sexual experiences are coming out of maturity and self-confidence.
> I am answering your questionnaire because I feel there are not enough statistics about women septuagenarians (I am seventy-eight), not enough understanding of the widow's situation. At my age and without responsibilities I do not want matrimony but I have a continuing sex drive which keeps me looking fifteen to twenty years younger

than my chronological age. Also, I had heart surgery two years ago, which has completely rejuvenated me. I want to live to the fullest extent of my capabilities.

I am sixty-seven, and find that age does not change sex much. Circumstances determine it. I have had much more sexual pleasure, both with my husband and other mates in recent years. I love not having menstruation.

(Hite, 1976: 508–510)

According to Rubin (1968: 88), the widespread acceptance of the myth of the "sexless older years" has a profoundly negative impact on the lives of the aged—"it makes difficult, and sometimes impossible, correct diagnoses of medical and psychological problems, complicates and distorts interpersonal relations in marriage, disrupts relationships between children and parents thinking of remarriage, perverts the administration of justice to older persons accused of sex offenses, and weakens the whole self-image of the older man or woman."

Just how typical is the plight of a 65-year-old man—self-described as having "a lot of pep" and "far from dead sexually"—who wrote to Ann Landers for sexual advice. Regarding his otherwise healthy 63-year-old wife, he wrote: "On my 63rd birthday, she did me the grand 'favor' of sleeping with me. She then announced that from now on I'd better forget about sex because, as she put it, 'It's obscene for a couple of old fools like us to carry on like newlyweds' " *(Globe,* November 30, 1977: 12).

Job Performance. As noted earlier, the public image of aging is generally associated with reduced capacity for job performance and diminished potential for development. In the 1975 Harris survey conducted for the National Council on the Aging, for example, it was determined that a majority of adult Americans agreed that old people are not very good at getting things done.

To examine worker characteristics as related to age, Bowers (1952) studied the personnel records including supervisors' evaluations of 3,162 workers between the ages of 18 and 76. A broad range of occupations was represented including foremen, minor executives, skilled craftsmen, operators of machinery, inspectors, clerks, and unskilled laborers.

Based on an index of worth consisting of the frequency of occurrence of favorable and unfavorable characteristics mentioned by supervisors for each employee, Bowers determined that older workers got higher ratings than their younger counterparts for attendance, steadiness, and conscientiousness. Moreover, no consistent age differences were found for job knowledge, dependability, accuracy, and emotional stability. Only on the characteristics of ability to learn and slowness did older workers get consistently lower ratings than younger workers. Overall, Bowers found that most workers over 65 "were considered very competent on the job and that they compared favorably with younger workers in the organization" (1952: 299). This finding has serious implications for the way mandatory retirement has been justified. If older workers have an undeserved reputation for poor job performance then their removal from the job must be due to some other force than a desire to have the best person on the job.

Intelligence. It is widely held that intelligence moves downward from early adulthood through old age. Not surprisingly, a majority of American adults questioned by Harris (1975) agreed that most people over 65 were not very bright and alert.

Indeed, many attribute childlike qualities to the aged. (Notice that similar childlike characteristics have also been associated with blacks and women. This is seen, for example, in the reference to blacks as boys and women as girls.) In a recent issue of a surburban small town newspaper, an article reported that the patients at a local nursing home "held their very own Christmas party." The article went on to indicate that patients "planned the party, made the invitations, decorated the cookies made by the chef, and took part in the entertainment, which included group singing of Christmas Carols." The article thanked a local drugstore for supplying "Santa's gifts." The intentions were admirable, but the message rang loud and clear. Old age is a period of "second childhood!"

As noted in Chapter One, gerontology has largely supported this stereotyped view of intellectual decline by their finding that different age groups actually differ with respect to I.Q. scores. Older groups often appear to come out on the short end, as far as intelligence is concerned.

But more recent, better-designed studies of intelligence and age strongly contradict the stereotyped view. Baltes and Schaie (1974: 35) reported "that the old man's boast, 'I'm just as good as I ever was,' may be true, after all." These researchers showed that earlier findings of intellectual decline in old age were an artifact of the cross-sectional method that compared one age group against another without controlling for generational differences. For reasons related to motivation, familiarity with terminology, and health, younger generations may in fact score higher on I.Q. tests than their older counterparts. But such generational differences may have nothing to do with chronological age per se. Consider, for example, the educational experiences 75-year-olds had when they were 15 and those which 15-year-olds are having now. Clearly, to the extent that I.Q. measures reflect these experiences, it would be unfair to compare the scores of one group with the scores of the other.

On the basis of longitudinal studies where the same individuals were measured repeatedly as they grew older, it became clear that intelligence doesn't necessarily decline—and may even increase—with advancing age. As a matter of fact, Baltes and Schaie report that only on one out of four measures of intelligence—what they call visuo-motor flexibility—did they find a definite decline. For two of the measures—crystallized intelligence and visualization—Baltes and Schaie discovered a systematic *increase* in scores from the first testing to the second, an increase that continued right into old age. Even people over 70 years of age improved. Jarvik (1979: 67) similarly indicates that "cognitive stability is the rule and can be maintained into the ninth decade, so long as illness does not intervene."

According to Birren (1968b), the belief that intelligence levels decline with age is partly a result of the way we calculate averages. "Mental decline in later years is not something that occurs in everyone a little bit, but it is irregularly distributed in the population such that a subset of individuals suffering from organic brain disease shows dramatic changes. If the tests of such individuals are averaged in with the population at large, as one does in a cross-sectional study, then one might mistakenly derive a rather smooth age curve. In fact, what occurs in individuals may be sudden changes after a substantially protracted plateau" (Birren, 1968b: 19).

Dramatic decreases in I.Q. test scores though unrelated to age per se have been associated with certain illnesses such as senile dementia and heart disease. Unfortunately, since old people are commonly expected to experience intellectual decline, their symptoms of what may in fact be illness are frequently passed over as being symptomatic of old age and therefore irreversible. As Siegler points out (1976: 55), "if you have a child who starts forgetting things, stumbling and falling over, you'll get that kid to a doctor fast. But if an older person starts forgetting things and starts stumbling over things, people ignore it. They say, 'Grandpa's getting old, don't bother him.' "

Conservatism.   One of the most pervasive stereotypes about old people involves their alleged conservatism or resistance to change. They are "set in their ways," so the popular saying goes. As reported by the Harris (1975) study, most American adults agreed that people over 65 were not very open-minded and adaptable. Even so insightful a writer as Simone de Beauvoir (1972) in her penetrating analysis of the degradation of the aged uncritically accepts the stereotyped view that aging is strongly associated with conservatism. She writes that "the old tend to join the ranks of the conservatives. It is hard for them to escape from the past that has formed them: They see the present through the medium of this past, and their understanding of it is poor. They lack the time and the means for adapting themselves to new circumstances, and their interests prevent them from even attempting to do so. They do their utmost to preserve the status quo" (de Beauvoir, 1972: 622).

The evidence linking age with conservatism is thin at best. In the area of political issues, for example, Pedersen's (1976: 152) study of more than 60 public opinion polls in California from 1960 to 1970, found "no general connection between age and resistance to change." In fact, change in public opinion surrounding the issue of fair housing in California occurred *most frequently* among those in the older age groups, while change related to the issue of a state lottery took place at about the same rate in all age groups. According to Pedersen (1976: 152) "the survey evidence from California suggests that the theory that there is a division of political labor in the electorate by which the young age groups provide flexibility and the older ones stability in the political system must be significantly qualified."

In the popular view, the presumed political conservatism of older people is frequently expressed in their "preference for Republicanism." However, Glenn and Hefner's (1972) study of Gallup postelection data spanning the 24-year-period 1945–1969 finds no evidence for the proposition that aging contributes to Republican party identification. On the contrary, "this study should rather conclusively lay to rest the once prevalent belief that the aging process has been an important influence for Republicanism in the United States" (Glenn and Hefner, 1972: 47). Generally, Glenn and Hefner's findings throw doubt on the stereotyped view that political conservatism increases with advancing age and instead supports the contention that older Americans have the capacity to participate fully in political change.

Glenn and Hefner show that from 1945 to 1969 Republican party identification increased and decreased among aging voters, but only as it increased and decreased among all voters. Thus, the aged changed their party identification when they believed it necessary. Only on one measure could it be said that the aged were conservative. They took somewhat more time to change their party identification than younger voters. But change they did, and at the same rate as their younger counterparts.

With reference to overall lifestyle, Palmore (1970) provides evidence that the aged are no more rigid or "set in their ways" than their younger counterparts. In his longitudinal study of 127 older persons from 1955 to 1967, Palmore found no evidence at all of advancing

age being associated with increasing persistence of lifestyle as indicated by sustained involvement in activities associated with health, family and friends, leisure, economics, and religion. On the contrary, Palmore found that persistence of lifestyle actually *declined* among older
men, and that it remained stable among older women.

   Disengagement. Very much like the popular image, the disengagement theory (Cumming and Henry, 1961) argues that the aging
individual accepts and even welcomes his withdrawal from society—
his reduced interaction, activity, commitment, and the like. According
to this view, "successful aging" is characterized by decreased social
interaction and emotional withdrawal from other people. As shown by
Tuckman and Lorge (1953a), most Americans have traditionally said
that older people "love life"; they like to "doze in a rocking chair."
The myth of disengagement goes hand in hand with stereotypes of
conservatism and intellectual decline to justify inequalities based on
age and deny the minority status of the aged—not only are old people
rigid and dumb, but they like being that way! (It is no coincidence in
this regard that blacks were similarly characterized as "happy-go-
lucky," until their massive protest activities during the 1960s.)

   The weight of evidence overwhelmingly contradicts the rocking chair thesis found in the theory of disengagement. Consider the
following representative findings.

   Palmore (1970) studied 127 volunteers aged 70 to 93 in a longitudinal study (four waves of interviews from 1955 through 1967),
finding no overall reduction in activities among men and only small
reductions among women (e.g., health, family and friends, leisure,
economic, and religious). Satisfaction decreased as activity decreased.

   Havighurst (1968b) reported that even among older persons
over 70, life-satisfaction tends to decrease as the level of activity decreases.

   Glenn and Grimes (1968) employed both cross-sectional and
longitudinal data on voter turnout and political interest to determine
that political interest typically increases from young adulthood to old
age.

   Gray and Kasteler (1970) found that 52 persons between 60
and 75 who for a period of one year became foster grandparents to
mentally retarded children expressed greater satisfaction with their
lives and were better adjusted than a control group of older persons
who had not participated as foster grandparents.

   Glenn's (1969) data from 35 public opinion surveys indicated
that the aged do not become less interested in national and interna-

tional affairs or become less willing to express opinions to survey interviewers.

According to Rose and Mogey's (1972) study of VA Normative Aging population, preference to early retirement increases with age—at the very time when social pressure to terminate the work role is most severe.

Cutler's (1973) data from the 1972 Center for Political Studies, American National Election Study, and the 1974 NORC General Social Survey found either stable or increasing levels of voluntary association membership through the age range 75+.

As noted by Bunzel (1972), the disengagement theory has been largely discredited. But it continues to provide a shabby rationalization for the maltreatment of old people in a youth- and task-oriented society and for the fear and hatred of old people as found among gerontologists and geriatricians themselves.

Cultural Aspects of Ageism

Acceptance of negative stereotypes about the aged is not confined to groups of youthful undergraduate students who expect to have little contact with older members of society. On the contrary, ageism seems to crosscut differences in age, region, social class, and occupation. According to Bennett and Eckman (1973: 575), "negative views of aging are shared by young and old alike." Studies have recorded agreement with age stereotypes among groups of physicians (Barrow, 1971), undergraduate occupational therapy students (Mills, 1972), ministers (Moberg, 1969), nurses (Wilhite and Johnson, 1976), graduate students (Tuckman and Lorge, 1953a), middle-aged children of aged parents (Wake and Sporakowski, 1972), institutionalized older persons (Tuckman and Lorge, 1952a), and even gerontologists (Arnhoff and Lorge, 1960).

As we have seen, ageism has persisted over many decades. Adult Americans of the 1970s typically accept very much the same public images of the aged as accepted by their generational counterparts of the 1950s and 1960s. The tenacious persistence and widespread acceptance of age stereotypes is a clue that ageism may be a cultural phenomenon—part of the normative order of the society in which it occurs. As such it is passed from generation to generation through the process of socialization much like other cultural phenomena—love of country and church, motherhood, the success ethic, and so forth.

As a cultural phenomenon, ageism is learned early in the life of a child beginning with experience with his parents and later his peers, teachers, and the mass media, and maintained throughout the life span. In an early study by Hickey, Hickey, and Kalish (1968), 208 third-graders wrote 2 or 3 sentences describing an old person. An analysis of the children's essays indicated that these third-graders were already aware of conceptions of old age. More than one-third of their written responses about the aged concerned ambulatory difficulties (for example, inability to walk, limping, or walking slowly) and almost another third concerned the generally feeble condition of the aged (for example, lethargy and frequent hospitalization). Typical statements were "my sister and I like to walk down to the corner with old Mr. Smith, but we have to walk slower when we are with him" and "old people usually die, or lose a leg or arm" (Hickey, Hickey, and Kalish, 1968: 229).

According to Seefeldt and others (1977), age awareness can be observed in three-year-old children. These investigators asked 180 children ages 3 to 11 to identify the oldest person depicted in a series of four photographs representing men of various ages. Even the three-year-old children correctly pointed out the oldest man from his photograph. Older children could also rank-order the men in the photographs in terms of age and accurately identify their ages. Seefeldt and others (1977) also sought to determine the stereotypes that children associate with aging. They found numerous images—overwhelmingly negative—many of which stressed physical appearance and health such as sick, ugly, sad, mean, wrinkled, short, sprained backs, and arthritis.

To view ageism as a cultural phenomenon is to recognize also that it varies from place to place and from time to time. Our society has not always mistreated or stereotyped its old people. Fischer (1977) argues convincingly that aged Americans living 200 years ago commanded respect, power, and privilege. Under Puritanism, old age was regarded as a sign of election and a special gift from God.

In their dress and hair styles, early Americans frequently tried to make themselves out to be *older* than they really were. Men would hide their natural hair beneath a wig, or they would powder their own hair to give it a white color associated with advancing age. Until the nineteenth century, the census-taker frequently found that citizens represented themselves as older than they actually were (Fischer, 1977). How our attitudes toward old age have changed! Today's census-taker frequently finds misrepresentation of age too, but in the opposite direction. Fifty-year-old women suddenly become 39; 76-year-old men are 70 again; and so on.

Ageism and Industrialization

In general, ageism flourishes under the social conditions imposed by industrialization (Cowgill and Holmes, 1972). The argument is that the privileged status of old people in preindustrial or agrarian societies is dependent on the knowledge they have accumulated over years of experience, and the power they maintain over extended family, government, religion, and the ownership of land. From a Marxian viewpoint, their status in many preindustrial societies is a consequence of an advantaged relationship to the means of production.

The position of the aged deteriorates under modernization. First, as levels of literacy and education increase, the members of society rely less on the older generation as a source of knowledge. Since the young are better educated, they hold a competitive edge with respect to jobs, status, and power. Second, retirement reduces the standard of living and social status of the aged. Third, the nuclear family becomes more prevalent, so that older members of society are expected to live apart in independent households or to seek institutional care. And, finally, in the shift from agriculture to industry, older members of society lose control over land and are forced instead to compete with younger persons for nonagricultural positions (Cowgill and Holmes, 1972).

Cowgill and Holmes's (1972) survey of the phenomenon of aging in many different societies, ranging from the most preliterate to the highly modern, suggests also a number of universals as well as variations. First of all, these investigators found that old age is universal, that is, all societies identify some people as old and treat them differently based on their age status. More specifically, old people everywhere tend to shift their roles from those requiring physical exertion to those demanding less strenuous physical activities. In modern societies, this shift entails movement toward formal retirement whereby disengagement or a cessation of all work activities is expected. But in less modern societies, old people are asked to pursue less strenuous yet equally or even more valued activities. In such preliterate societies, old men who are no longer expected to be warriors or hunters are instead *promoted* to advisory and supervisory positions. They are expected to become priests, headmen, or elders. As Cowgill and Holmes suggest, the net result is to generate and maintain high regard for the elderly.

> In all of the African societies, growing old is equated with rising status and increased respect. Among the Igbo, the old person is assumed to be wise; this not only brings him respect, since he is con-

sulted for his wisdom, it also provides him with a valued role in his society. The Bantu elder is 'The Father of His People' and revered as such. In Samoa, too, old age is 'the best time of life' and older persons are accorded great respect. Likewise, in Thailand, older persons are honored and deferred to and Adams reports respect and affection for older people in rural Mexico. Apparently, this was the situation in the traditional culture of the Pima Indians, although it is now being undermined by changes in land tenure, urbanization, and the superior education of the children (1972: 310).

Ageism in Colonial America. Most observers agree that the forces of industrialization contribute to the level of ageism in society. However, Fischer (1977) suggests that negative attitudes toward the aged were already increasing *before* the growth of urbanization and industrialization in American society had begun. The structure of the American economy changed very little before 1790, yet the great transition in age relations was already underway.

Fischer (1977) argues that cultural forces underlying the American War for Independence also formed the basis for changes in relations between young and old. More specifically, a revolution in attitudes toward age took place between 1770 and 1820, at a time when many hierarchically oriented institutions declined, and the ideal of equality emerged in full force. As applied to legal status, social conditions, and political rights, equality called into question the existing hierarchies of sex, race, and age. As a result, the elderly began to lose their privileged status in America.

Liberty is another cultural ideal that may have been involved in the declining status of older Americans. The concept of liberty reduced the authority of old age by destroying the communal ties of the aged to the family, the church, and the town. The growth of individualism in America served to loosen the obligations between young and old and instead contributed to "a spirit of social atomism" (Fischer, 1977: 63).

Many changes occurred in the social structure and attitudes of colonial America: preferential seating arrangements for the aged were eliminated; mandatory retirement laws appeared; youthful fashion was preferred; age preference shifted away from old age to youth; and eldest sons lost their inheritance advantages.

Ageism Not Present in All Industrializing Societies. Palmore and Manton (1974) have presented evidence recently to suggest that as societies move beyond an initial stage of rapid modernization (during which the employment status of the aged temporarily declines), the socioeconomic status of the elderly may actually increase. When modernized societies mature, their rate of change levels off, so that educational and agricultural gaps between young and old decrease. Moreover, such societies create institutions to replace the farm and family in preserving the status of the aged (for example, retirement benefits, retraining, legal codes to protect the aged, and so on).

It should also be emphasized that industrialization—even in its transitional state—does not necessarily bring about decline in the status of old people and the growth of ageism. As reported by Palmore (1975), the case of Japan suggests persuasively that a tradition of respect for elders can be maintained in the face of extremely advanced levels of industrialization. Consider the specific circumstances of the Japanese elderly. They are well integrated into their families, most of them continuing to hold household functions and to live with their children. Most continue to be employed, unless they stop for health or voluntary reasons. Their health status has markedly improved in terms of nutrition, sanitation, and medical care. In addition, Japanese society has institutionalized a number of nationwide customs, programs, and occasions in which regard for the aged is symbolized:

1. Respect for the Elders Day is an important national holiday;
2. the sixty-first birthday is used to express affection for the aged and to honor them;
3. forms of deference toward the aged such as bowling and honorific language are commonly observed;
4. regulations give priority seating to the aged in buses and trains;
5. all older Japanese are eligible to receive a minimum income from the government; and
6. free medical care is given to most elderly Japanese.

According to Palmore (1975), the relatively high status of Japanese elders was maintained by a longstanding tradition of respect for age and aging. The basis for this tradition is twofold: first, a vertical social structure which obligates younger persons to respect all older persons; and, second, filial piety which obligates children to honor their own parents and grandparents.

With reference to a vertical social structure, Japanese society is characterized by a hierarchy of relationships involving superiors and inferiors (for example, between parents and children, masters and servants, or teachers and students). Some ranking by seniority almost always occurs in all Japanese relationships—even in those between friends and colleagues. The emphasis on seniority is a basis for the vertical society and, specifically, for the persistence of the high status of Japanese elders.

Filial piety has its roots in Confucian precepts as well as in ancient ancestor worship. According to Japanese religious beliefs, dead ancestors acquire Godlike powers that determine all worldly events and human actions. Moreover, the happiness of the living is dependent upon the effectiveness with which they respectfully serve the dead. Hence, the tremendous devotion of the Japanese to dead ancestors and to older members of the family who will shortly become dead ancestors.

Russia provides another exception to the rule that modernization reduces the status of the elderly. McKain (1972) reports that almost all Russian elders

1. are given the opportunity to play useful and active roles in society;
2. live in the homes of their children or friends; and
3. have the economic means to continue the lifestyle they had led as younger members of society.

Ageism and Mass Communication

As an agent of socialization, mass communication plays a central role in the transmission and perpetuation of prejudice. Television, in particular, has consistently assigned negatively stereotyped roles to blacks and women, or has ignored them altogether (Gerbner and Gross, 1976), and it appears that the aged have received no better media treatment than have other minorities. As revealed in his study of characters appearing in prime time network television drama between 1969 and 1971, Aronoff (1974) reports that the aged comprised less than 5 percent of all characters, about half of the proportion that they actually occupied in the population of the United States at that time. What is more, when they did appear as dramatic characters, the aged tended to be depicted as evil, unsuccessful, and unhappy. "In a world of generally positive portrayals and happy endings, only 40 percent of older male, and even fewer female characters, are seen as successful, happy, and good" (Aronoff, 1974: 87).

Television commercials have similarly ignored or stereotyped the aged. For example, a content analysis by Francher (1973) determined that only 2 out of 100 television commercials contained older characters. The focus of attention was on "the Pepsi Generation"— young and attractive characters who were featured in order to promise youthful appearance or behavior. As Hanaver (1976: 12) recently noted, "it's the rare wrinkled face—and never a wrinkled hand—that appears on television ads. Even the denture glues go for younger folks;

the laxative ladies seldom go beyond middle age, if that, and judging from the ads, no one over 35 ever cleans house except 'Aunt Bluebelle.' "

Age stereotypes are an element of the portrayal of old people in prescription-drug advertisements as well. In a content analysis of drug ads in the physician-oriented journals, *Medical Economics* and *Geriatrics*, Smith (1976) found that aged models in these drug ads tended to be stereotypically depicted. They were frequently described solely on the basis of old age as disruptive, apathetic, temperamental, and out of control. The importance of Smith's results are underscored by the fact that drug ads seem to have a substantial impact on the behavior of physicians (Linn and Davis, 1972). To what extent are such ads responsible for the negative attitudes toward the aged held by many of them?

Theories of Prejudice and Ageism

Applying the minority concept to the aged raises the interesting possibility that the social and psychological factors associated with prejudice and discrimination against racial and religious minorities also help to explain the situation of the aged in America. As a form of prejudice, ageism may be a result of the personality needs and social functions in society that can be satisfied by attacking, ignoring, or neglecting vulnerable groups that have been socially defined as inferior or as evil.

Psychological Sources of Ageism

At the psychological level, prejudice may have *ego-defensive* consequences, providing a safe outlet for displaced aggression and aiding in the protection of self-esteem. For an individual who does not wish to acknowledge threatening or painful truths about himself, a minority group may become a negative point of comparison against which his values, abilities, or performances can be regarded as superior (Levin, 1975). From this viewpoint, certain individuals—those who are excessively concerned with their status and the maintenance of their self-esteem—express a generalized hostility directed against the members of any group regarded as weak, powerless, or inferior (Adorno and others, 1950).

Based on their stereotyped public image as declining, sexless, and disengaged, and their vulnerable position in our society, we might suspect that aged Americans would be disliked by the same individuals who hate members of other minorities, and for the same reasons. To find out, Kogan (1961) asked 482 undergraduate students for their agreement/disagreement with a number of statements concerning attitudes toward ethnic minorities, blacks, the mentally ill, the blind, the deaf, and the crippled. He found that subjects who held unfavorable attitudes toward old people also tended to be prejudiced toward the members of ethnic, mentally ill, and physically disabled minorities. These data support the contention that "there is a general trend for subjects to be positively or negatively disposed toward a wide variety of groups deviating in some respect from a hypothetical norm of similarity to self" (Kogan, 1961: 53).

Kogan also asked his subjects to respond to Srole's (1956) Anomie Scale, whose items have previously been found to be correlated with prejudice against ethnic minorities. His results suggest that subjects unfavorably disposed toward the aged are also more likely to be anomic; that is, they are more pessimistic about the future, feel helpless in the face of powerful social forces, and feel incapable of finding meaning or purpose in their lives. In short, anomic individuals have a precarious and threat-oriented view of life. According to Kogan, they may regard old age as a period of life when an individual is least able to deal with a hazardous environment. Hence, their negative evaluation.

Social Sources of Ageism

Aside from its psychological consequences, prejudice also has a part to play at the sociological level. The realities of economic scarcity and group conflict help to influence the character of the relationship between minority and majority, including their attitudes toward one another.

Prejudice against racial and religious minorities frequently has a rational economic basis, occurring as the minority-group member attempts to secure a share of the scarce resources of his society. For example, antiimmigrant nativist activity has tended to increase during periods of economic depression. "The Native American party of the 1830s, the Know-Nothing Order of the 1850s, the American Protective Association in the last two decades of the nineteenth century, and the scores of antialien, one-hundred-percent-American groups in the 1930s—these all show the tendency to try to bolster a shaky economic situation by prejudice against recent immigrant groups" (Simpson and Yinger, 1972: 116).

Some observers have suggested that ageism (not unlike sexism and racism) has been perpetuated by a ruling elite in order to serve its own economic interests. Simone de Beauvoir (1972) argues, for example, that the exploiting class seeks to weaken the economic strength of the working class by reducing the solidarity between young workers and old retirees. According to de Beauvoir, negative age stereotypes are elements of bourgeois thought that serve to project an image of the aged as a group that is different. The result is a disunified working class whose members lack the means for protecting or enforcing their rights.

Whether or not it is part of some deliberate plot concocted by the members of one group to exploit another, ageism is undoubtedly related to economic scarcity and conflict. As Friedenberg (1969) argues, conflicts between young and old over scarce economic opportunities create a social climate within which negative age stereotypes flourish.

The role of industrialization may be crucial in this regard. In contrast to farming, industrialization is marked by shifting job opportunities and recurring recessions and depressions that create competition for available jobs. One method of creating jobs for young workers is to eliminate old workers from the labor force on the grounds that they are rigid, unproductive, and slow to change. The courts have frequently agreed. In 1975, for example, the United States Supreme Court affirmed the constitutionality of a Louisiana law that required civil service workers to retire at 65. In its decision, the Court stated that mandatory retirement is important for maintaining an efficient and vigorous civil service and providing a method for promoting younger workers (Schulz, 1976).

Recent federal legislation has opened opportunities for continued employment for numerous Americans in their sixties who formerly would have been forced into retirement and were unprotected by age discrimination laws. With respect to government jobs, the new law totally eliminates mandatory retirement. Unfortunately, for the private sector, this legislation reaffirms the right of government to impose an arbitrarily assigned compulsory retirement age. We will return to examine the implications of this law in Chapter Five.

Gerontophobia

Psychological and sociological factors that have previously been applied to explain the development of prejudice against racial and religious minorities seem also to fit the case of ageism. But prejudice against the aged also has causes not shared by other varieties of prejudice. Bunzel (1972) has chosen to refer to the unique aspects of ageism as *gerontophobia*—the unreasonable fear and/or hatred of the elderly. Gerontophobia seems to occur, first of all, because most young people will someday be old, and, secondly, because old age is associated with death. In either case, there is a strong element of avoidance, whereby the young person denies the inevitability of his fate—whether death or old age—by regarding the aged with intense hostility. According to Bunzel, gerontophobia is a malady that afflicts 20 percent of the population of the United States. (However, Palmore (1972) has suggested instead that it is a rare occurrence, being only one form of the much more pervasive phenomenon of ageism.)

Atchley (1977) correctly notes that being old is in itself a stigma that may reflect in part the fact that in our society death typically occurs during later life.

> In other societies, where death rates are high, people die at all ages, and death is thus considered something separate from old age. But in societies with low death rates most people survive into later life and death thus becomes associated with later life. Because of this association, young people may shun older people, who remind them of their own mortality.
>
> (Atchley, 1977: 18)

Another factor in the development of gerontophobia is the American value-orientation that regards nature as an obstacle for human beings to overcome (Kluckhohn and Strodtbeck, 1961). This cultural view is expressed in the popular conception of the aging process as a disease to be investigated and eventually eliminated by human intervention (Rosenfeld, 1976).

On the positive side, our belief that we can dominate nature has made possible important medical discoveries that have enhanced the quality of life. Unfortunately, old people have come to be seen as the victims of a disease that has thus far eluded manipulation and control, but which will someday be conquered.

A vicious circle operates at the value level. Based on negative stereotypes about their incompetence, the elderly are encouraged—and in some cases required—to disengage. Yet they continue to be evaluated in terms of cultural values emphasizing future-orientation and economic productivity. Members of our society are rewarded for their economic utility, but the limited access of elder Americans to opportunities for achievement keeps them at a distinct disadvantage with respect to social status (Rosow, 1974).

In contrast to stable, tradition-oriented societies, American culture emphasizes innovation and change. As a result, the aged cannot play a valuable role as symbols of historical continuity or respected tradition. They are therefore trapped in their status by a value system that stresses achievement and change but, at the same time, singles them out as a special group whose members can be denied opportunities for achievement.

According to Rosow (1974), the status of the elderly would be markedly enhanced by a basic change in our values—a change that would reduce the influence of the Protestant ethic. In an alternative status system based on "intrinsic human qualities, people could be evaluated and rewarded for their attributes and relationships rather than for their performances" (Rosow, 1974: 153).

However, as recognized by Rosow (1974), massive transformation of the values influencing social status is unlikely to occur in the foreseeable future. There is little evidence that social values have changed in any significant way despite the predictions of the last decade of a "greening of America" and a revolution of consciousness.

Summary

Old people in American society constitute a minority group whose members are victims of ageism. For decades, there has been widespread acceptance of negative stereotypes about the aged involving references to their intellectual decline, conservatism, sexual decline, lack of productivity, and preference for disengagement. Though most such images are based on half-truths or outright falsities, they continue to be used to justify the maltreatment of the aged by American society.

Ageism is a cultural phenomenon whose acceptance is longstanding and crosscuts differences in age, region, and social class. Ageism is passed from generation to generation by means of socialization. Children very early come to recognize age differences and to evaluate others based on their age. The mass media socialize members of society to accept negative age stereotypes by depicting older people as evil and unsuccessful or by ignoring them.

Some theories of prejudice against racial and religious minorities also seem to help explain the situation of the aged in America. Persons who hold unfavorable attitudes toward the aged also dislike blacks, the mentally ill, and the physically disabled. Such persons tend to be anomic, expressing a threat-oriented view of life.

Ageism may also be a result of economic competition between

young and old for scarce jobs and privileges. Industrialization may have created the conditions necessary for intense forms of ageism.

As a unique phenomenon, prejudice against the aged may also reflect an element of avoidance, whereby the young person denies the inevitability of his fate and takes a hostile posture regarding old people in society.

Chapter Four

Reactions to Ageism

In the face of widespread prejudice and discrimination, society asks minority-group members to play a role; that is, to fulfill a set of expectations that, if carried out, would set them apart from others and maintain their subordinate status in society. For example, in the area of race relations, Pettigrew (1964) has identified the role of Negro—a cluster of norms traditionally applied to all black Americans, requiring that they act out the part of inferior in their relations with whites.

Similarly, women in American society traditionally have been expected to behave in accord with what Kluckhohn and Strodtbeck (1961) call "Variant Value Orientations"—those intellectual, aesthetic, and moral concerns "which busy men so often define as the nice but non-essential embroidery of American life" (1961: 356). The role of Negro and the stereotypical role of woman are echoed in what can be called the role of senior citizen.

The Role of Senior Citizen

Not unlike the more obvious forms of racism and sexism, ageism has long been a fact of life to which older Americans have had to adjust their self-images as well as their lifestyles. Older persons have been the unfortunate recipients of age-related expectations. Many of these serve to separate them from other members of society, if not to degrade and humiliate them.

Expectations for old people are based on negative age stereotypes. Members of American society generally expect and even encourage the aged to be asexual, intellectually rigid, unproductive, ineffective, and disengaged. Senior citizens are supposed to stay out of the way, sit in their rocking chairs, and enjoy the golden years. They are expected to be inactive, invisible, but happy.

An important element in what we refer to as the role of senior citizen is its lack of *prescriptions* for behavior, rules for what ought to be done, and its emphasis on *proscriptions*, rules for what ought not to be done. Thus, old people are not supposed to hold jobs, to have sexual interests, to engage in sexual intercourse, or to marry. Unfortunately, the role of senior citizen fails to specify exactly what old people are supposed to do instead—except to suggest very vaguely that they find substitute activities for those they have lost and to prepare for death (Rosow, 1974; Wood, 1971).

So lacking in socially approved alternatives is the role of senior citizen that retired individuals may become "imprisoned in a roleless role" (Burgess, 1960). In this regard, Blau (1973) notes that many problems associated with age are actually a result of the "role exits" that occur in old age. Most individuals over 65 are expected to lose significant roles, typically through retirement or loss of control over the household.

Of course, it is true that role losses occur throughout life and not only during old age, as, for example, when an individual finishes high school or leaves a job. But role exits prior to old age frequently lead to new valued roles that replace those being relinquished. For example, many people go from one job to another or make the transition from high school to college. By contrast, the role exits associated with old age typically are not followed by entry into other socially valued roles. Instead, role exits in old age "terminate a person's participation in the principal institutional structures of society—the nuclear family and the occupational structure" (Blau, 1973: 18–19).

Given the diversity that characterizes the population of older Americans, it should come as no surprise that their reactions to the role of senior citizen are also very diverse. Faced with expectations of behavior that are particularly unpleasant to fulfill, older people may react by acceptance, avoidance, and/or aggression.

Acceptance

Minority group acceptance of prejudice and discrimination may range from reluctant submission all the way to wholehearted endorsement (Lincoln, 1961). For example, prior to the civil rights movements of the 1950s and 1960s, many black Americans felt that it was sensible to accept what they could not change or avoid. Most blacks in the South used jim-crow buses and restrooms when alternatives were unavailable; some black servants accepted the racial epithet "boy" in order to keep their jobs. And prior to emancipation, the childlike "Sambo" personality was skillfully employed by black slaves in order to secure rewards from their masters, and to minimize their own suffering (Thorpe, 1971).

Although such instances of acceptance usually have been carried out with the most extreme reluctance, some black Americans have internalized the expectations of their inferior status, actually welcoming subordination as part of the natural order of things. When this occurs, such self-hatred represents a form of mental illness (Lincoln, 1961) and has resulted most often in the acceptance by black Americans of the negative stereotypes perpetuated by white Americans (Banks, 1972). Beginning with early childhood, both blacks and whites learn to associate black with dirty, bad, and ugly, and white with clean, nice, and good (Proshansky and Newton, 1968).

As with blacks, varying degrees of internalization of a role can be seen in the personality patterns of the aged uncovered by Havighurst (1968a). Based on his analysis of 59 men and women aged 70–79, Havighurst reports finding a few subjects whom he calls the *successful disengaged*—older people who have voluntarily reduced their role commitments and activity levels, at the same time maintaining much satisfaction with life. These old Americans, few in number though they may be, have willingly accepted the role to which our society has assigned them. "They have high feelings of self-regard, with a contented 'rocking chair' position in life" (Havighurst, 1968a: 23). Less motivated forms of acceptance are represented in what Havighurst identifies as *apathetic* and *disorganized* personality patterns in the aged. Both of these have low role activity, but low levels of life satisfaction as well.

It is probable that those old persons who are enthusiastic about playing the role of senior citizen have internalized that role in much the same manner as they are socialized to accept other conceptions of desirable and undesirable behavior. After all, the old were once young, at which time they were exposed to institutionalized notions of appropriate behavior for the elderly. Additionally, they have been primed to relinquish middle-aged roles long before their actual termination. For as expectations for competence gradually decline as one ages, the individual receives an increasingly larger share of negative sanctions for doing exactly the same activities for which he or she was rewarded earlier in life (Riley and others, 1969).

Subtle but important sanctions may be present in the most innocent-looking everyday situations. Anthropologist Ashley Montagu (1977: 49) illustrates by personal example: "I've appeared on dance floors where it was quite obvious that younger people resented my presence because I was 'a grey-haired old man' who didn't belong there. There's real rejection, as if they want to tell me, 'Act your age.' "

Self-Fulfilling Prophecy

Particularly damaging for those aged who accept whole-heartedly society's prescriptions and proscriptions on aging is the operation of self-fulfilling prophecy. Thus, young people are socialized to accept negative age stereotypes and to expect the role of senior citizen. As a result, they discourage, even punish, any behavior on the part of the aged that is active, effective, or competent. In turn the aged come to accept the negative stereotypes and to act in accordance with the role of senior citizen.

Consider the ideas about sexual interest and activity among the aged. For too many, the sexless older years become a self-fulfilling prophecy. It thrives in the face of overwhelming evidence to indicate that sexual desire and capacity continue into old age. The ultimate result is a reduction in the level of what might otherwise be regarded as normal, healthy, sexual behavior. Because they have swallowed the line that sex is exclusively for the young, many of the aged are hesitant to admit having sexual motives, or they feel guilty, ashamed, or embarrassed about engaging in sexual relations (McKain, 1972; Rubin, 1968). Others may fear being ridiculed by younger persons. One psychiatrist, for instance, reported two cases in which children sought to have their aged parents committed to a mental hospital because they were living with members of the opposite sex (Lobsenz, 1974). Such behavior, of course, reinforces the stereotype and can be used by those who seek to confirm the assertion that sex is unimportant in the lives of the aged.

Montagu talks about self-fulfilling prophecy as carried out by those who have accepted the role of senior citizen:

> Most older people have a way of acting as if they were older. They're playing a role. This role of the aged has not only been imposed by others upon them, but is self-imposed. They think, "I'm this age, so I have to behave this way." They feel they must say, "Oh well, when you're my age . . . " or "When I was your age . . . " that sort of thing, to emphasize the fact that they're older. This perception of a difference between the old and the young comes not only from the perceptions of the young, but from the older person who, by his behavior, accepts the definition of being old (1977: 49).

Jacob's (1974) study of the relatively well-to-do retirement community he calls Fun City uncovered an important group form of acceptance of the role of senior citizen. Perhaps half of the 5600 residents of Fun City claimed they settled there to retire. "By this they mean to withdraw for the most part from the society of others, watch television, read, play an occasional game of cards, and walk the dog" (Jacobs, 1974: 80).

Many followed through on their intention. Only a small minority of them became active participants in Fun City's club activities. According to one estimate, approximately 25 percent of Fun City's aged never even left their homes. Acceptance was the rule rather than the exception.

The Aged and a Leisure Ethic

Even the desire to accept the role of senior citizen in its most attractive form may turn out to have negative consequences for the individual. Imagine the appeal of believing that when we grow old we will be able to relax and play 100 percent of the time. We have often wished we could do just this during the most boring or demanding work days in our youth and middle age. As an alternative to the extremely negative, unattractive, images of old age, the idea of old age as a sort of ultimate vacation draws many of us. However, as Miller (1965) has pointed out, an older person who wishes to enjoy his or her leisure must justify that leisure. In our instrumental, work-oriented society, we say we go on vacation or enjoy games or recreation in order to relax. We play so we may continue to work, to be more efficient and useful. There is no available leisure ethic that applies readily to the leisure activity of old people. For them, leisure is not a means to an end; it is the end in itself, and so is not valued in society. Many people who retire expecting to enjoy leisure as they did when they were younger are severely disappointed at the negative social definition of their leisure that they have brought with them into old age.

Acceptance as Resignation

We must be careful not to exaggerate the extent to which wholehearted acceptance characterizes the responses of old people to their assigned status. The vast majority of them probably comply with extreme reluctance to a situation which they detest but feel powerless to change or avoid. As Rose (1965b) points out, older people are pushed out of jobs, formal and informal associations related to jobs, and even leadership positions in voluntary associations. They regret the drop in role activity, but accept it as an inevitable accompaniment of growing old or as an aspect of our society that cannot be changed.

Acceptance and the Retirement Community

An important appeal of the retirement community—one frequently ignored by those who study the reasons for its widespread presence—is to separate old people from the prejudice and discrimination of young people. Fear of victimization and violence is often given as a reason for moving to a retirement setting (Jacobs, 1974). But the more subtle impact of ageism may also play a part. The everyday indignities experienced by the elderly in their dealings with the young can be minimized in age-segregated communities, where almost everyone shares the stigma of aging and seeks to avoid its most painful consequences. But of course isolation also contributes to the belief that the aged are a separate or different kind of people from the rest of society and reduces the visibility of people who are exceptions to the stereotypes of old age.

Avoidance

Certain minority-group members attempt actively to avoid the consequences of their minority status by passing for members of the majority group or by refusing to accept their status and attempting to maintain positive self-images. For example, light-skinned blacks have passed for whites; Jews have passed for Gentiles by changing their names or giving up religious rituals.

In a similar way, the denial of old age may serve as a defense mechanism employed by the elderly to avoid the negative role of senior citizen. Many avoid thinking of themselves as old for as long as possible (Drevenstedt, 1976; Tuckman and Lorge, 1954; Taves and Hansen, 1963). As Bernard Baruch used to put it, "Old age is always 15 years older than I am."

Surprisingly, perhaps, the chronological age of persons over 65 does not seem to be related to whether they see themselves as elderly (Zola, 1962). In a study of 1700 older residents of Minnesota, Taves and Hansen (1963) found that more than 40 percent first considered themselves old at 80 or over, and 13 percent said they never thought of themselves as old. Only 5 percent thought of themselves as old at 65.

In a recent Harris (1975) survey, people 65 and over voiced a strong preference to hear themselves referred to as senior citizens or as mature Americans, while they expressed a strong dislike for designations such as an old man or old woman, an aged person, or a golden ager.

In some senior citizen clubs, the members are fined if they use the word old. "Before new business, the president calls for left over business. It is as if being old is a disgrace" (Jacobs and Vinick, 1977: 2).

Denial of old age is a form of avoidance, but it is not necessarily to be avoided. Given the severe stigma of aging and the negative connotations associated with it, a middle-aged self-concept may actually sustain morale and increase satisfaction with life. As Peters (1971: 71) notes, "the acceptance of an older self-image may be tantamount to the acceptance of (or resignation to) the fact of an old status."

Very clearly, many persons over 65 who regard themselves as old or as elderly are not so satisfied with life or so emotionally well adjusted as those who continue to consider themselves middle-aged (Phillips, 1957; Taves and Hansen, 1963). What is more, Bell's (1967) study of 55 residents of homes for the elderly indicates that socially uninvolved or disengaged individuals tend to classify themselves as old, whereas individuals who remain socially active avoid the self-designation of old age.

Avoidance and Ageism

Avoidance may frequently indicate successful adjustment to old age, but it also minimizes possibilities for organizing to end ageism. Individuals over 65 who conceal their age are generally unwilling to attribute their economic problems to ageism. Relatively few of them admit that ageism is a very important influence in their own lives, though they may see it as an important factor in society at large (Kahana and others, 1977).

A case in point is found in Percy's (1974) discussion of the efforts made by the elderly of Watertown, New York, to organize during the late 1960s. The first name proposed for their group—the County Council on the Aging—was rejected because many members objected to the use of the word aging. The group was finally able to settle on calling themselves the Senior Action Council. Another " . . . ticklish problem was persuading still-active farmers, sixty-five and older, that they should join. 'Age has no relevance to them' says one organizer. 'We had a hell of a time convincing them they're old people and should join an old people's organization; they still work a fourteen hour day' " (Percy, 1974: 102).

Re-engagement

A positive form of avoidance is for the aged to *re-engage*—to substitute new roles for the old roles they have lost. Jacobs and Vinick (1977) have reported the experiences of 78 old people who became either re-employed or remarried after the loss of a job or a spouse. According to Jacobs and Vinick, their subjects were average men and women representing all walks of life " . . . who exhibited the kind of capacity for growth and new activities in later life that we believe to be much more widespread than has been recognized" (1977: 1).

Re-engagement may be found where it is least expected to occur. Jacobs's (1974) study of Fun City revealed that numerous residents of this retirement community were employed in part- or full-time jobs, despite the absence of civil service, major retail stores, or other institutionalized forms of employment. Several residents worked in the local post office or newspaper; some were employed as realtors and part-time college professors; many donated their time to charities.

The need for re-engagement was emphasized by the large number of Fun City residents who worked at jobs whose requirements were far removed from their preretirement occupations:

> Retired admirals paint houses, retired colonels pump gas or transcribe math problems into braille for the blind, while housewives act as realtors. Other well-to-do residents work as handymen or gardeners, or in a neighboring town at a discount department store. While it is true that most Fun City residents live on fixed incomes and work to supplement these, many others who work for poor pay at unskilled jobs are independently wealthy.
>
> (Jacobs 1974: 26)

Passing

Passing is frequently expressed in the consumption by the aged of products designed to give the appearance of youth or middle-age. Witness the tremendous growth in the use of cosmetics, hair pieces, face-lifts, wigs, weight-control items, and fashion-conscious clothing. This emphasis on personal appearance can be seen in Boucheron's (1959) *How to Enjoy Life after Sixty*, when he urges men over 60 to have their straggly gray hair trimmed at least every two weeks. "It adds ten years to their age otherwise" (1959: 54). He also suggests a face-lift in order to delay the "look of age." And for men over 70, Boucheron makes the following suggestion:

> Watch the grease spots on your ties, on your coat lapels. Remember the old saw about the "untidy old man with part of his breakfast on his

vest." If you cannot afford to have your suits dry-cleaned frequently, clean the spots with inexpensive dry-cleaning fluid. Clothes which are neatly pressed and clean give you a well-kept appearance and prove to the world you still care how you look. It all adds up to keeping young (1959: 55).

People over 65 who regard themselves as young or as middle-aged may not be expressing a mere bias or delusion. Older people in good health may continue to feel as strong and vigorous as they did during earlier periods of their lives. However, as Butler (1975: 14) points out, "the problem comes when this good feeling is called 'youth' rather than 'health,' thus tying it to chronological age instead of to physical and mental well-being."

Avoidance and the Retirement Community

As we have seen, the residents of retirement communities frequently accept the role of senior citizen (Jacobs, 1974). However, Hochschild's (1973a) study of Merrill Court, an "old-agers commune" near the shore of San Francisco Bay, indicates that acceptance is not the inevitable product of an age-segregated lifestyle, especially when it develops outside of institutional settings. Hochschild argues instead that the autonomy and involvement of old people may be sustained by a community of appropriate peers. In Hochschild's study, "the widows of Merrill Court took care of themselves, fixed their own meals paid their own rent, shopped for their own food, and made their own beds; and then did these things for others" (1973: 55).

Hochschild characterizes the relationship among residents of Merrill Court as *the sibling bond*, by which she means an exchange of goods and services based on a shared age status that places all residents in the same boat and that provides a meaningful existence independent of their children.

As Hochschild notes, Merrill Court hardly represents an ideal situation for old people. Like so many programs and policies, it is essentially an adaptation to bad social conditions and therefore contains elements of acceptance. But the sibling bond at Merrill Court provoked much greater independence and activity than does the kind of relationship associated with institutional living. The residents of institutions are patients who in childlike fashion are forced to depend on attendants and nurses for the satisfaction of their everyday needs. The relationship between patient and attendant is nonreciprocal. It is one-way. No wonder that individuals living in traditional types of institutions for the aged are especially likely to accept the negative age stereotypes that society has assigned (Tuckman and Lorge, 1952a). By contrast, the sisterhood experienced by residents of Merrill Court rests on adult autonomy and exchange. "This is what people at Merrill Court have and people in institutions do not" (Hochschild, 1973a: 55).

Avoidance as Destructive Behaviors

As we have seen, avoidance of the role of senior citizen can be found in the efforts of old people to deny their age and stay young. To this point, we have stressed those forms of avoidance in which the aged remain engaged (or re-engaged) and active, or attempted to maintain their middle-aged self-concept. Such avoidance behavior generally has the effect of moving the aged toward the younger members of society with respect to their interaction patterns, their values, or both. But avoidance also occurs among old people who have given up on our society or on life itself. We turn our attention now to consider the more unfortunate forms of behavior that some older individuals express in order to avoid playing the role of senior citizen. These forms move the aged away from the young by exaggerating differences, providing a basis for isolation, or terminating the relationship. Ironically, they often serve to reinforce and support the very stereotypes that the aged seek to avoid. Specifically, we focus on senility, alcoholism and drug abuse, and suicide.

Senility.   It has become abundantly clear that some older persons diagnosed as suffering from irreversible Organic Brain Syndrome are needlessly functioning at a "vegetative level" for lack of treatment (Settin, 1978). In this regard, gerontologists have also raised the interesting possibility that cases of senility of an apparently organic nature (for example, due to deterioration of cell structure) may actually represent a form of refusal to accept the aged status (Payne, Gibson, and Pittard, 1969). According to this hypothesis, when it comes to the move from middle age to old age, each individual chooses whether to accept or reject the aged status. Psychological rejection may result in a psychotic state whose patterns are modeled after those of organic psychotics who are of similar age and subculture.

The circumstances of suffering have been observed to provoke infantile behavior not unlike that which is symptomatic of senility in the aged. To take an extreme example from Bettelheim (1943), the behavior of many concentration camp inmates included:

1. disappearance of conversation about sexuality;
2. loss of control over excretory functions;
3. silliness;

4. unpredictable changes in mood;
5. unstable relationships;
6. boastfulness regarding accomplishments in their former lives; and
7. anti-Semitism.

According to Elkins (1959), characteristics similar to those of concentration camp victims developed among slaves in the southern United States.

The symptoms of avoidance psychosis may be indistinguishable from those of its organic counterpart. As a result, physicians may frequently misdiagnose cases of senility that, based on behavior alone, they assume to have an organic basis. Or they may never think to raise the possibility that observed physical conditions of an aged patient may be a result rather than the cause of psychological problems (Payne, Gibson, and Pittard, 1969).

Despite the stereotyped conception of the senile aged, organic senility does not appear to be an intrinsic element of the aging process. People have lived a century or more without ever experiencing senile brain dysfunction. And symptoms usually associated with senile behavior such as chronic forgetfulness and incompetence in performing simple tasks actually occur among only 5 percent of the population of Americans over 65 (Zarit and Kahn, 1975). Butler and Lewis (1973) have noted that brain autopsy often reveals no sign of organic degeneration in people diagnosed as senile, while finding organic change in people who were never so diagnosed. In some societies where the elderly have high status, symptoms of senility may be virtually absent (Shelton, 1965.)

Note that while the intent of senile psychosis may be avoidance, its result is to reinforce or support the popular age stereotypes in which old persons are viewed as operating in a period of mental and physical decline. Thus, from the viewpoint of society, senile behavior has all of the characteristics of acceptance: Old people doing exactly what old people are expected to do—being forgetful, childish, self-centered, and impulsive.

From the standpoint of medical practitioners, the diagnosis of senility justifies the use of psychotropic drugs as a means of controlling the behavior of older patients and helps explain why psychotropics are so commonly prescribed for the elderly. As Arluke and Peterson suggest:

> By managing behavior in this manner, the cause of the problem is attributed to the older person; it is the individual that we seek to change. By focusing on the symptoms and defining them as senile

psychosis, we ignore the possibility that their behavior is not an illness, but an adaptation to a social situation. It is the "victim" who is being blamed and not the social system. Attention is thereby diverted away from the family or the institution; the notion that the problem could be a social structural one is diffused. Thus, the medical perspective of diagnosing illness in individuals lends itself to the individualization of social problems (1977: 18).

Since the label senile dementia or organic brain dysfunction defines the older person as irreversibly ill and therefore beyond rehabilitation, it also becomes justifiable to remove physically the elderly for purposes of treatment and control (Ciliberto, 1980). As Frankfather has asserted, this diagnosis serves to legitimize their removal to nursing homes, where the emphasis is on efficient and economical maintenance—"if they are 'senile,' it does not matter where they go" (1977: 190).

It should be emphasized that less severe forms of illness than psychosis may also turn out to have an important component of avoidance. No one knows how many of the illnesses associated with old age have been caused or exacerbated by a desire for escape from the role requirements of the aged status. As Parsons (1960) suggests, illness may serve as an escape hatch for old people who have been excluded from opportunities to be productive and are defined as useless. They can rationalize their uselessness through the incapacitation of illness (Arluke, Kennedy, and Kessler, 1979). What is more, many lonely older people cannot psychologically afford to lose their symptoms of illness, lest they give up their relationship with a physician (Lipsitt, 1977).

Alcohol and Drug Abuse.   Alcoholism or drug dependence that begins or increases during old age may also represent forms of avoidance. (This has certainly been true in the case of racial minority groups, for whom the level of consumption of liquor and drugs is high [Simpson and Yinger, 1972].)

Alcoholism afflicts more than 15 percent of the aged population (Zimberg, 1974). In addition, it is well established that physicians frequently prescribe tranquilizers for old people who commonly complain of anxiety-related symptoms (Butler and Lewis, 1973). Unfortunately, the use of drugs and alcohol may too frequently constitute a long-term means whereby individuals attempt to cope with the problems associated with growing old in America. And, as in the case of functional senility, the outcome of excessive drug or alcohol usage may be to reduce mental and physical activity, thereby supporting the very stereotypes which old people seek to avoid.

Suicide. Suicide is avoidance at its extreme. Suicide extremely high among people over 65, especially among men, to be associated with the frustrations and isolation of old age (Bock, 1972; Butler and Lewis, 1973).

The actual incidence of suicide among the aged is difficult to determine. Explicit cases can be counted with relative confidence; but we have no way to know just how many old people encourage self-destruction via discontinuing medical treatment for illnesses, refusing to follow a nutritious diet, losing their appetite, or causing "accidents" to occur (Payne, Gibson, and Pittard, 1969).

Why Avoidance?

What accounts for the widespread presence of forms of avoidance among the elderly? As Riley and others (1969) point out, socialization to new roles requires the presence of clear expectations as well as positive incentives. In order to assure compliance, then, the role of senior citizen should contain the equivalent in respect to any of the other major roles associated with adulthood. There must be something in it for the aged—there must be something available to give the old person a sense of usefulness in a society where usefulness is valued. Nothing of the sort could be said to characterize the negative and ill-defined expectations currently associated with old age in America.

Compulsory retirement may be a major factor in the desire of old people to avoid the role of senior citizen. As noted by Cavan (1962), retirement separates an individual from his previous roles, without providing him with the motivation for a new self-concept. First of all, when an individual is compelled to disengage from society, he no longer has the means to carry out whatever social roles he formerly played (the individual becomes a bookkeeper without books, a machinist without tools, and so on). Second, the retired individual is isolated from his former coworkers. Third, he no longer sees respect and approval in the evaluations of others (expressed in such language as "He is done for, an old-timer, old-fashioned, on the shelf"). Fourth, he cannot accept the new self-image, since it is of lower valuation than the old self-image that has been part and parcel of him for many years.

In a sense, refusal to acknowledge old age is also a form of acceptance—not necessarily of the old age designation on a personal level, but of the larger views of our society regarding the aged. Many old people seek to escape the effects of age discrimination. At the same time, however, they may also accept the same age stereotypes that younger people do. As Rosow suggests, "old persons depreciate other aged persons and in the same terms" (1974: 81).

Aggression

It has been suggested that Western society may be entering an era of social change in which the struggle for "age rights" occurs on a large scale (Neugarten, 1970). From the standpoint of old Americans, such a struggle would depend upon the heightening of aggression as a response to their aged status.

In contrast to avoidance, the aggressive response seeks not to deny the role of senior citizen but to eliminate it. This involves the alteration of social definitions and social forces. If this were to occur, the behavior of older individuals would exist in the absence of any age-related expectations. Clearly, continued involvement in society would not then be seen as a form of avoidance. Consciousness of kind is critical. The aged status must be recognized and repudiated, so that individuals can take pride in being old and become aggressively militant.

Rose (1965b) was early to recognize that the aging subculture is to some extent also a contraculture, emerging out of the need to combat age discrimination and containing elements of opposition to the status quo. A key factor is frustration. Old people who are dissatisfied with their lives and have poor filial relationships express significantly more hostile attitudes toward the young than do those who are satisfied with life and have good filial relationships (Cryns and Monk, 1972). More importantly, perhaps, support for organized political activity on behalf of the aged tends to increase among older persons who perceive the aged to possess low prestige in our society (Cutler, 1973). It may be significant to note in this regard that a recent survey of older persons in Michigan found that more than half perceived their financial status to be inadequate and deteriorating (Peterson, 1972). According to a recent survey, a majority of the 107,000 readers of *Retirement Living* magazine expressed their displeasure with images of the elderly as depicted by television. These readers described media images of old people as ridiculous, decrepit, and childish (Hanaver, 1976).

As demonstrated by the middle-class student protests of the 1960s, political activism does not require that its proponents experience severe poverty. With reference to the aged, Neugarten (1970) argues instead that aggressive forms of group consciousness may grow as old people become increasingly educated to the fact that their low status in our society is attributable to the widespread acceptance of ageism and age discrimination. Thus, ageism may turn out to be its own worst enemy.

It is possible that ageism toward the old may take more overt forms in the near future and may be countered by action on the part of older people. For one thing, there are segments of the society in which old people are becoming a visible leisure class. While a proportion of the present old are disadvantaged in terms of education as well as income, numbering many foreign-born and many who have spent their lives as unskilled workers, future generations of old will be quite different: Better educated, healthier, longer-lived, in higher occupational levels. As they become accustomed to the politics of confrontation they see around them, they may also become a more demanding group. There are signs that this is already so, with, for example, appeals to "senior power" (in some ways analogous to the appeal to "black power"), and with more frequent newspaper accounts of groups of older people picketing and protesting over such local issues as reduced bus fares or better housing projects. Whether these incidents will remain isolated and insignificant, or whether there is an activist politics of old age developing in the United States is a debatable question, but it would be a mistake to assume that that which characterized the political position of the old in past decades will be equally characteristic in the future.

(Neugarten 1970: 17–18)

Collective efforts to reduce the impact of (if not to eliminate) the role of senior citizen can be found in the activities of organizations such as the National Council of Senior Citizens, the American Association of Retired Persons, the National Retired Teachers Association, and the National Association of Retired Federal Employees. Representing millions of older people, such organizations have informally associated themselves with the major political parties and have taken public positions on issues affecting the aged (for example, on Medicare). As a result of effective lobbying on the part of organizations representing the interests of old people, the Senate Special Committee on Aging recently was given permanent status.

However, it should be stressed that at least some of the major activities of traditional organizations for the aged have focused on making the best of a bad situation. In particular, they have provided old people with discount drugs, libraries on aging, driving courses, newsletters, group insurance plans, and travel packages—goods and services that may aid the aged in adjusting to their assigned status in society, but which do little if anything to change it (Binstock, 1972).

Individual political effort too has tended to focus on measures to ease the adjustment of the aged. Where the aged have used the ballot box in an effective manner, they have successfully gained taxi service, cafeteria space, permission to build elderly apartments, senior citizen buses, and special tax breaks.

Recently, however, organizations such as the Gray Panthers have more directly sought to change the role of senior citizen by stressing "Senior Gray Power" and by demanding an end to discriminatory practices such as mandatory retirement. The Panthers see themselves as a movement of social activists who seek nothing more or less than to control their own lives. They include young people as well as old who believe that problems experienced by the elderly are an expression of more fundamental defects in the structure of our society. The Panthers attempt to raise the age-consciousness of young and old through seminars and public speaking (Offir, 1974).

Aggressive movements have begun to attract their culture heroes. At recent hearings before the House Select Committee on Aging, numerous successful elders spoke in favor of the repeal of mandatory retirement laws. Among those present were Colonel Harland Sanders, the 86-year-old fried chicken king; Ruth Gordon, the 80-year-old Academy Award winner; Averell Harriman, the 86-year-old former New York Governor; S. I. Hayakawa, the 70-year-old semanticist turned Senator; Frances Knight, the 71-year-old director of the United States Passport Office; Susanna K. Cristofane, the 78-year-old mayor of Bladensburg, Maryland; and Tommy Corcoran, the 76-year-old Washington attorney. What is more, groups of elderly Americans have come together to protest or demonstrate—sometimes in the streets of major cities—in order to dramatize their plight or protect their interests. In Boston, demonstrations by thousands of old people persuaded city officials to effect a rollback of fare increases in public transportation. In Philadelphia, hundreds of old people demonstrated against proposed cutbacks in social security payments during a visit by the Vice President. A probe of nursing home abuses by the Chicago Area Council of Senior Citizens resulted in the closing of 15 substandard nursing homes. In Houston, a political action group of old people was organized to achieve reduced fares in city buses. A proposed Medicaid cutback was eliminated in New York state when thousands of its elderly residents protested. In Michigan, old people physically blocked traffic at dangerous intersections until traffic signals were installed. In New York City, several hundred old people demonstrated at city hall to force city officials to provide a tax abatement for landlords of apartments occupied by elderly tenants with rent exemptions.

As the number of aged in our population continues to grow, we may expect that their aggressively militant activities will increase as well. Eighty-three-year old Major Roy Nordheimer who serves as an advisor to the Chicago Area Council of Senior Citizens has warned that "there is an increasing feeling among our people that if we can't get what we need, we'll have to be more drastic" (Percy, 1974: 109).

Summary

American society asks minority group members to play a role; that is, to fulfill a set of expectations that separate them from others and maintain their subordinate status. Old people are asked to play the role of senior citizen. They are supposed to stay out of the way, sit in their rocking chairs, and enjoy the golden years. Unfortunately, the role of senior citizen is based on negative stereotypes, lacking socially approved alternatives. The reactions of the aged to their assigned role in society contain elements of acceptance, avoidance, and aggression.

Acceptance may range from reluctant compliance to enthusiastic endorsement. A particularly harmful product of whole-hearted acceptance is the operation of self-fulfilling prophecy, whereby the aged come to accept negative age stereotypes and to act in accordance with them. Frequently, however, what appears to be enthusiastic conformity may actually be reluctant compliance with expectations that old people feel powerless to change or avoid. It was noted that an important appeal of the retirement community is to minimize the indignities experienced by the elderly in their everyday dealings with the young.

Avoidance occurs when the elderly attempt to deny or conceal their old age. Many individuals avoid thinking of themselves as old for as long as possible and express a preference for designations such as senior citizen or mature American. Some attempt to pass by consuming products designed to give the appearance of youth or middle-age.

An important form of avoidance is re-engagement whereby the aged substitute new roles for the old roles they have lost (for example, remarriage or re-employment). They may also attempt to maintain independence and activity rather than to accept the dependency of an institution for the aged.

Avoidance also occurs among old people who give up on society or on life itself. Senility, alcoholism and drug abuse, and suicide may represent symptoms of avoidance behavior that move the aged away from the young by exaggerating differences, providing a basis for isolation, or terminating the relationship.

In contrast to avoidance, forms of aggression seek not to deny the role of senior citizen but to eliminate it. The aging subculture is to some extent also a contraculture, developing out of the need to combat discrimination and containing opposition to the status quo.

Collective efforts to reduce the impact of the role of senior citizen are to be found in the activities of organizations that represent millions of old people. Some of the activities of such organizations have traditionally focused on easing the adjustment of the aged to their status in society. Recently, however, organizations such as the Gray Panthers have more directly sought to encourage Senior Power and have demanded an end to age discrimination. What is more, groups of elderly Americans have begun to protest or demonstrate in order to dramatize their plight and protect their interests. Such militant activities on the part of the aged are likely to increase.

Chapter Five

Proposals and Prospects for Change

As indicated in Chapter Two, many of the programs designed to aid the aged can be characterized as exceptionalist in viewpoint. That is, they concentrate their efforts on ameliorating the symptoms of a problem, while ignoring the social, economic, or political conditions that make such programs necessary in the first place. With reference to the aged in America, exceptionalist programs often seek to educate, socialize, or otherwise modify the characteristics of old people or enable them temporarily to survive in a hostile environment.

With respect to the reactions of old people to ageism, exceptionalist programs and policies seem frequently to focus on helping them achieve acceptance or avoidance: some aim at easing the adjustment of old people to the role of senior citizen; others help old people to avoid that role.

Encouraging Acceptance

Programs directed at easing acceptance typically include measures to make life more pleasant for those individuals who are willing to comply with social expectations and institutional arrangements associated with growing old in America. Even a partial list is a long one: Senior Fun buses, discount coupons for theaters and restaurants, age-segregated housing, special cafeteria space, birthday and Christmas parties for nursing home residents, Medicare, Old Age Survivors' Insurance, meals on wheels, senior picnics, group dining programs, student volunteers in retirement centers, self-protection courses, and programs to provide gifts for Christmas.

An increasingly popular arrangement for easing acceptance is the retirement community that is age-segregated and situated for the sake of recreation or leisure. Jacobs's (1974) description of Fun City provides an appropriate illustration. This community of old people was located in "a warm valley, about ninety miles southeast of a large metropolitan area, where the prevailing winds are such as to keep it relatively free from smog" (Jacobs 1974: 1).

Thus, Fun City was geographically isolated from urban life. It was not a suburb of a large metropolitan area and contained no industry. This setting may have stimulated leisurely activities, but it also minimized employment opportunities and reduced contacts with younger members of society.

Even the best-intentioned programs may contain elements that encourage acceptance of the role of senior citizen. Consider proposals for preretirement training that are meant to minimize the shock of compulsory retirement and to prepare the employee for the postwork period. Such programs assume that significant numbers of older individuals will continue to drop from the labor force. Universities, labor unions, and businesses offer preretirement courses, often at no charge, in which issues related to nutrition and health, financial planning, leisure activities, and living arrangements are discussed. One large department store has begun to set up annual interviews with each of its employees from age sixty to retirement (Albrecht, 1969).

Encouraging Avoidance

Programs designed to help the aged avoid their assigned role have benefited numerous old people. An important example can be found in proposals to counteract the self-fulfilling prophecy of intellectual decline, whereby old people sometimes act in accordance with societal expectations and fail to develop any further, or to maintain their intellectual capabilities. Because of the prevailing stereotype depicting the aged as intellectually incompetent, little emphasis has been placed on the need to provide them with educational stimulation or facilities. However, education could be organized not just for youth, but the entire life cycle. In particular, education for the aged could be planned and executed with the participation of old people, so that it directly relates to their needs and goals. Important aspects of their education might include helping to define aging in more positive terms and providing old people with a broader range of opportunities.

Volunteer programs involving retirees represent a particularly successful effort at moving the aged from acceptance to avoidance. For example, the Foster Grandparents Program, initiated in 1965 and funded by the Office of Economic Opportunity, presently includes more than 13,000 older men and women who serve some 27,000 children in all 50 states, the District of Columbia, and Puerto Rico. They typically work in state institutions for the retarded, child-care centers for children from single parent homes, with children in need of foster homes, or in public school systems with special-needs children. Some also work with handicapped children in private homes, small community centers, and local guidance centers.

In return for engaging in loving and supportive interaction with these children, foster grandparents typically receive a small (if not token) weekly income supplement, a daily hot meal, and transportation expenses. In addition, they are given a sense of dignity, the elevation of self-esteem, and the security of really being needed.

As another example, the Service Corps of Retired Executives and Active Corps of Executives have some 6,000 older volunteers who offer free assistance and counseling to small businesses and community organizations throughout the nation (*AARP News Bulletin*, 1977).

Many programs to help the aged have the effect of substituting one form of avoidance for another. A particularly successful illustration of such a program is provided by Manaster's (1972) account of the experiences of a group of "confused," "disoriented," and "withdrawn" patients—all 75 years or older and regarded as senile—who participated in group therapy sessions for a period of several weeks. The stimulation provided by this group experience made a dramatic difference in the lives of these aged. They gradually became willing to verbalize complaints about their treatment by others and developed important friendships as well. Patients who were previously unwilling to leave their floors began planning trips to concerts and other social events. Patients who were previously uncommunicative began to carry on fluent conversations.

Acceptance, Avoidance, and Social Change

To the extent that they help to ease the burden of growing old in America, policies and programs stressing acceptance and avoidance serve a useful function for individual aged. Without such programs, many more old persons would surely suffer from hunger, boredom, ill health, and poor self-esteem.

Unfortunately, some acceptance- and avoidance-oriented programs may also operate at the expense of older Americans. For example, volunteer programs aid needy business and community projects and help fill the idle hours of a small proportion of the aged. But such programs also downgrade the economic value of the aged by encouraging them to donate the very services for which younger persons are well paid. In a society where individuals define one another largely on the basis of income or wealth, volunteer activities do little to enhance the status of the aged. Additionally, an exclusive emphasis on acceptance and/or avoidance may also serve to weaken efforts at achieving basic change in the social conditions of the aged. Many of the most successful of these programs operate at the expense of system-change behavior—behavior that seeks to change the role of senior citizen.

This may happen in two ways. First, those individuals who successfully participate in programs to avoid or accept the aged status are less likely to want change because they are less likely to identify their problems with ageism or regard themselves as being old. For example, if preretirement training actually helps to ease the transition from employment to retirement, then those who are trained should better accept retirement and be less willing to work to eliminate it.

A second way in which exceptionalist programs retard system-change behavior is to reward continued acceptance and punish (or withhold rewards from) failures to comply. For example, Medicare helps to cover the cost of hospitalization and nursing home care for the aged, but it fails adequately to pay for their care at home. Thus, an old person who falls ill and relies on Medicare coverage may be better off economically being institutionalized than having to pay the cost of visiting nurses, home health aids, or visiting homemakers. From the standpoint of the taxpayer, the cost of hospitalizing an aged individual frequently exceeds the cost of maintaining home care. The cost is great from the standpoint of the aged person as well, for to meet the requirements of Medicare he or she must give up autonomy and assume a position of total dependence in an institutional setting (Jones, 1977).

Influencing System-Change Behavior

As we have seen, programs aimed at acceptance and avoidance are frequently effective with respect to short-term goals. However, for the sake of long-term improvement in the status of the aged, we propose that more attention be paid to increasing system-change behavior on the part of young and old alike.

From the standpoint of institutional change, we must determine where to break into, and reverse, the vicious circle that characterizes the circumstances of growing old in America. Ageism and age discrimination support one another, assuring the continuance of the role of senior citizen. Negative stereotyping about the aged justifies the poor treatment accorded them; discrimination leaves the aged in a vulnerable position that further reinforces negative attitudes.

The Mass Media and Ageism

The mass media occupy a central position in the perpetuation of the vicious circle of ageism and discrimination. Acting as a mirror of our culture, the media frequently reflect the pervasive cultural influence of negative attitudes and stereotypes about the aged. Thus, relatively few old people appear in leading or star dramatic roles, on quiz programs, or in commercials; and when they do appear, they are often portrayed as villainous, unsuccessful, or unimportant. This treatment helps perpetuate negative public images of the aged.

Ageism and Institutionalized Care

The relationship between ageism and discrimination is vividly illustrated in the case of nursing homes for the aged. The social organization of nursing homes has a good deal in common with that of hospital wards and mental institutions dealing with the aged:

1. patients are relatively powerless, low-status individuals whose prognosis is regarded as poor, and whose credibility is low;
2. turnover, absenteeism, and poor role performance are common among employees who occupy marginal positions in the labor market, and such workers staff many positions in nursing homes; and
3. treatment is seen as custodial rather than as therapeutic.

(Stannard, 1973)

Butler (1974) recently charged the United States Social Security Administration with participating in a cover-up, whereby the results of nursing home inspections are concealed from public view. He urged individuals to harass the Social Security Administration until deficiency reports were made available. But he also realized that such patchwork measures merely ease the adjustment of the aged to their assigned role, while ignoring basic issues regarding the legitimacy of that role in society.

Butler is correct in arguing that "there must be fundamental reform in the care of the aged, using quite different facilities than now available" (1974: 530). He suggests establishing comprehensive campus-type centers—both residential and outreach—that are graded in terms of patient need and that focus on returning the patient to full participation in the community.

The evidence is piling up that many institutionalized older persons could be cared for outside of hospitals and nursing homes if comprehensive health and social services were available to them. Unfortunately, funds are generally available only for institutional care and not for coordinated home services (Markson, Levitz, and Gognalons-Caillard, 1973).

This preference for institutional care is in some part a reflection of a much broader, longer-standing social trend whereby the family unit has relinquished more and more of its responsibilities to other specialized, more efficient institutions such as day-care centers, charities, hospitals, nursing homes, and the like (Parsons, 1960). But the institutional sanctioning of nursing-home care also reflects a social psychological phenomenon—the tendency for Americans traditionally to deal with what they consider deviant behavior by distancing themselves from it. Consider the widespread presence of total institutions to deal with poverty, illness, crime, and old age. Institutions such as prisons, mental hospitals, reform schools, public housing, nursing homes, and retirement communities segregate people and their problems—the existence of which "respectable" Americans have not wanted to face. Only under the impact of worsening economic conditions have community-based methods for dealing with deviance received widespread public support. Home-based care for the elderly is no exception.

L.I.F.E. It must be added that there are times when institutionalized care for the aged is appropriate, and in such situations group consciousness among residents of institutions takes on particular importance. For example, in Massachusetts, Edward Alessi and Ric Dancey founded L.I.F.E. (Living Is For the Elderly), an organization of some 250 institutionalized residents from at least 40 nursing homes. They seek to "put the 'I' back into their lives, such as Independence, Initiative, Involvement, Interest, and Image of One's Self." L.I.F.E. objectives emphasize the necessity for raising the age consciousness of both nursing-home residents as well as community members. Specifically, L.I.F.E. seeks to

1. bring nursing-home residents and community members together,
2. allow residents of different nursing homes the opportunity to come together,

3. meet on a regular basis to discuss problems and find solutions, and
4. educate both community people and nursing-home residents to the potential and strengths of the elderly.

Changing How We Care for the Aged.   Profound change in the nature of care of the aged—especially those who are disabled—may depend upon first reducing ageism and age discrimination in other areas of life as well. In the ideal situation, enhancing the status of old people would assure that those who work with old people have higher status and income as well. Reducing the impact of negative age stereotypes would increase the autonomy of the aged in their relationships with agencies and institutions. Increasing economic opportunities for the aged would increase their power and their status. Treating old age as a normal, valued, stage of life apart from dying and death would foster a therapeutic approach and discourage the view that nursing homes are custodial institutions where old people go to die (Markson, 1971).

Retirement as a Form of Age Discrimination

Reversing the vicious circle of ageism depends very much on eliminating pressures toward retirement so that the aged have the same employment opportunities as other adult Americans do. In turn, economic power will change the negative stereotypes of the aged portrayed by the mass media. As more old people remain employed and their purchasing power increases as a group, they are more likely, for example, to be selected as quiz show contestants, and to be assigned favorable treatment in commercials. This is exactly what happened to media images of black Americans as they became viewed as a profitable market (Lerner, 1957).

As employment opportunities for the aged grow, their interest in education as a way to get better jobs and higher income will increase. In the past, the lack of job possibilities for the elderly resulted in their failing to take advantage of the educational opportunities available to them, and in the stagnation of their intellectual abilities—a process that reinforced negative stereotypes of the aged. Prospects for employment would provide a much needed incentive for the aged to pursue education and to maintain or improve their intellect.

Reducing Pressures Toward Retirement

Recent federal legislation has amended the 1967 Age Discrimination in Employment Act to cover employees until age 70. Despite the good intentions of many congressmen and citizens who oppose mandatory retirement on humanitarian grounds, the major impetus for such legislation has come from a realization that we may no longer be able to support the Social Security benefits of a growing population of older Americans.

Whatever the motivation, this legislation clearly benefits people between 65 and 70 who previously would have been forced to retire, regardless of personal preference or ability. However, by reducing the number of old people who are forced to retire to those over 70, it also redefines old age from a legal standpoint. Ironically, the result may be to reduce the effectiveness of Senior Power as a realistic strategy for producing basic change in the status of the aged.

Senior Power depends on amassing large numbers of old people who vote a self-interested bloc. It depends also on mobilizing the organizational effectiveness of traditional voluntary associations of old persons, many of whose active members have traditionally been 60 or over. Under the recent modification in compulsory retirement laws, such persons may be far less likely to see their interests as coinciding with those forced to retire. Persons between 65 and 70 may be inclined instead to avoid the aged status and to reduce their participation in organizations representing such interests. Thus, the long-term impact of recently modified compulsory retirement legislation may be to worsen the prospects for improving the circumstances of those Americans over 70 who continue to suffer from discrimination without the benefit of protective legislation.

Factors Maintaining Retirement

The total elimination of forced retirement would be but a first step in the reduction of age discrimination, comparable in its consequences to the part played by the abolition of slavery in the history of the civil rights struggle of black Americans. But even as the abolition of slavery did not mark the end of racial discrimination, the elimination of mandatory retirement laws would not mark the end of age discrimination.

In our society, retirement has become so profoundly associated with old age that most people over 65 continue to give up their jobs, whether or not the law requires them to do so. Everything con-

spires against their continued employment. In the first ⸝
Americans apparently do not love their work since they
retire long before the age at which mandatory retirement la\
them to do so. This seems to be especially true for blue-collar   ⸝⸝s.
For instance, just 2 percent of the blue-collar workers employed by
General Motors continue on the job long enough to reach mandatory
retirement age.

Additionally, many companies exert pressure on older workers
to get them to retire. Age discrimination laws notwithstanding, em-
ployers have been known to make life miserable for workers who re-
fuse to retire when they have outlived their usefulness to the company.
Just as it is difficult to prove discrimination based on race or sex, so it is
frequently hard to demonstrate conclusively discrimination by age.

A third factor implicated in the persistence of retirement involves a self-fulfilling prophecy whereby older workers accept the
appropriateness of their disengagement and begin to play the role
expected of them. Charles Whipple (1977) of the *Boston Globe* has
identified retirement as being a prime culprit in such behavior—

> I've seen a number of employees who, if it weren't for approaching
> retirement, would continue to be loyal and efficient workers. Because
> of it, they have lapsed into premature senility. They walk around like
> Zombies just waiting for the day they retire (1977: 26).

A final factor in the appeal of retirement is the economic incentive provided by government programs such as Old Age Survivors'
Insurance (Social Security). The concept of a social security system
for the aged originated in the 1880s in Germany under Chancellor Otto
von Bismarck, who sought to reduce unemployment among young
German workers. When the United States Social Security System
began in 1935, the age of 65 was selected as a minimal age criterion for
eligibility.

In effect, our system of social security has rewarded those who
retire and has withheld benefits from those who continue to engage in
full-time work. After the age of 65, social security has been tied to
chronological age per se rather than directly to disability or inability to
find work. This may have made sense during the Great Depression of
the 1930s or before the turn of the century when relatively few people
lived beyond age 65. However, given the large and growing number of
healthy, viable elders in today's population, there is no good reason to
maintain a form of assistance that discourages productive activity and
equates aging with disability. On the other hand, it would be disastrous
to propose the abandonment of social security without considering

alternative forms of assistance that protect people of *any* age who are disabled or unable to find employment. As we shall see, those programs which *affect* the aged may frequently be preferable to those programs *for* the aged.

Proposals for System Changes

The 1971 White House Conference on Aging focused its efforts on developing a national policy on aging. Numerous recommendations came out of the conference, many of which would require fundamental changes in our system and in the attitudes of the younger members of our society. The conference proposed, for example,

1. that the educational curricula from nursery school through college be designed to increase understanding of the aging process;
2. that more vigorous efforts be made to eliminate age discrimination in employment;
3. that continued employment or retirement with adequate income be made a matter of choice;
4. that alternatives to institutional care be developed; and
5. that older people be given opportunities for independence, usefulness, and growth.

Senior Power: the Gray Panthers

A central issue for the aged concerns the absence of control and independence in their lives. In retirement, many of the aged have been forced to rely upon forms of public assistance. In nursing homes and hospitals, they have depended upon a staff of nurses, physicians, orderlies, and administrators who make daily as well as longer-term decisions for them. How might these circumstances be changed?

The militant Gray Panthers offer a program of system-change priorities that if instituted would deal a serious blow to the forces of age discrimination and ageism. The Panthers advocate:

1. participatory democracy for all aged residents in institutional settings;
2. effective and inexpensive mass transportation systems;
3. enactment of a national health-care program through a public corporation;
4. abolition of compulsory retirement for all age groups;

5. a national program of housing integrated with respect to age, income, and race; and
6. inexpensive educational programs to meet the needs of people of all ages.

Enactment of the Gray Panther priorities would change the role of senior citizen. The aged would no longer reside in segregated settings such as retirement communities, would no longer be dependent upon federal or state assistance programs that single them out for special treatment, and would no longer be required to give up productive, useful roles in our society.

Earlier, we saw that the minority-group model suggests that system-change behavior must be initiated by older Americans themselves who recognize their common problems and come together in a shared quest for equality. However, some have argued the futility of any senior power strategy based on political pressure such as by bloc voting. They suggest instead that organizations of old persons have been effective in the past only with respect to publicizing the plight of the aged, and gaining for the aged a larger share of funds from existing programs. From this viewpoint, no drastic movement toward equality for older Americans is seen as likely to occur (Atchley, 1977; Binstock, 1972). Similarly, during the 1960s, gerontologists argued the foolishness of discussing attempts to raise the retirement age in the face of chronic unemployment and increasing demands for a shorter work week (Slater, 1963). Yet the 1970s witnessed popular legislation to increase the age of compulsory retirement, at a time of worsening unemployment. We feel senior power has great expectations.

Senior Power and the Young

Even militant old-age groups such as the Gray Panthers count on enlisting the aid and cooperation of the young in a shared struggle for human liberation and social change. Indeed, there may be certain issues around which young and old might effectively pool their resources and form temporary alliances. Therefore, programs designed *for* the aged should be carefully separated from those programs that *affect* the aged. The former (for example, Medicare and Supplemental Security Income) are aimed directly and exclusively at the problems of the elderly; the latter provide benefits for a broad range of individuals including, but not limited to, the elderly (Gold, Kutza, and Marmor, 1976).

Support for programs *for* the aged may be difficult to secure from the members of younger populations, many of whom would prefer to deny the aging process in themselves and perceive the elderly as a competitive force. Even more detrimental is that such age-entitlement programs are exceptionalist in scope; they tend to perpetuate the image of elders as constituting a group apart from other members of society. Consider, for example, benefits provided through programs under the Older Americans Act. Under Title IV of the Act, considerable research in the field of aging has been supported. Unfortunately, much of this research has focused on characteristics of the aged as reviewed in Chapter Two rather than on characteristics of society that may be fundamentally responsible for the mistreatment of elders. Under the Older Americans Act, Title VII, group dining programs for older persons have been developed. While such programs have obviously benefited numerous elders, they unfortunately fail to move beyond the goal of easing the adjustment of old people to their assigned role in our society and therefore can do little if anything to improve their situation.

In sharp contrast to programs for the aged, programs that *affect* the aged may be broadly perceived as benefiting young as well as old, and these should constitute the basis for the alliance between young and old. For example, the Medical Assistance Program (Medicaid) finances medical services for public assistance recipients. Only 20 percent of the Medicaid recipients are aged 65 and older, but they consume some 39 percent of the benefits. Another program that *affects* the aged is the Food Stamp Program—a negative income tax directed at reducing the cost of food. Eligibility for food stamps depends only on income and family size, not on age. In 1974, estimated food stamp benefits to the elderly totalled $95 million (Gold, Kutza, and Marmor, 1976). In the future, then, we might expect coalitions of young and old to come together for the sake of programs that *affect* the elderly such as national health insurance or a guaranteed annual income.

Raising the Consciousness of the Aged

Despite the opportunities for alliances across age groups, it would be unduly optimistic to assume that the young will consistently tolerate, let alone support, efforts on behalf of the aged. As employment restrictions are lowered, for example, the interests of old and young are bound to come into direct conflict.

This has already been observed to happen among college students who see their employment opportunities as being in short supply. In 1977, for example, a senior at the University of Massachusetts who was looking for a job in journalism was concerned enough about a repeal of mandatory retirement laws that he wrote an angry article for the *Boston Globe*. In his article, the student argued that the elimination of mandatory retirement would decrease the availability of jobs and opportunities for promotion. In order to justify his position on more than a self-serving basis, he also argued that ending forced retirement would reduce the flow of fresh ideas, maintain employees whose judgment begins to fail and who slow down, and upset pension plans.

To be effective, therefore, any movement of older Americans must begin with consciousness-raising activities. The minority-group model suggests that this is a three-part process.

In the first place, members of our society who reach 65 or 70 must begin to regard themselves as sharing a common social status by virtue of their age (for example, old, aged, or elderly). Secondly, they must also recognize the presence of ageism and age discrimination in their personal lives. And finally, they must reverse the pejorative connotations associated with aging, so that old age becomes regarded as a normal, desirable stage of life (as Edward Alessi recently remarked, "Elders must find their Africa").

The task is, of course, an enormous one. By present-day standards, to suggest that old could be beautiful or even neutral is to suggest a profound change in our standards. Yet the precedent exists. Consider the situation of black Americans prior to the civil rights movements of the 1950s and 1960s. At that time, the connotative meaning of the word "black" was overwhelmingly negative, and many black Americans preferred being referred to as colored or Negro. However, the three phases of consciousness raising outlined above have influenced numerous black Americans since the 1950s. They have become very much aware of their brotherhood with other black Americans; they identify the source of their common problems in the racism of white America; and they preach if not practice, the virtues of blackness.

Clearly, the experiences of minority groups such as blacks and women may be useful as a guide for predicting the course of consciousness raising as it occurs among the aged. Just as clearly, however, the uniqueness of old age as a stage in the life cycle must be considered as well. Whites never have the opportunity to become blacks; men rarely become women. By contrast, the aged draw their entire population from the young who have been socialized as *majority-group members* to accept negative stereotypes and feelings about old age. Upon reaching 65, they join the minority group and must disabuse themselves of ideas learned over a lifetime. As a result, age consciousness-raising may be particularly difficult to achieve.

The aged are in a unique position as a minority group. For those members of society who have not yet reached 65, age consciousness raising means, above all, the recognition of the inevitability of their own aging, a recognition that they too may ultimately benefit from whatever changes occur in the status of the aged. Given the competitive nature of our society, there are very few such parallels in the relationship between men and women or between whites and blacks.

Bibliography

AARP
1977   News Bulletin, March, 18(3):5.
Adorno, T. W., Else Frankel-Brunswick, Daniel J. Levinson, and Nevitt H. Sanford
1950   The Authoritarian Personality. New York: Harper and Row.
Albert, William C., and Steven Zarit
1977   "Income and health care of the aging." Pp. 120–126 in Steven H. Zarit (ed.), Readings in Aging and Death. New York: Harper and Row.
Albrecht, Ruth
1969   "The family and aging seen cross-culturally." Pp. 27–34 in Rosamonde R. Boyd and Charles G. Oakes (eds.), Foundations of Practical Gerontology. Columbia, South Carolina: University of South Carolina Press.
Allen, Fannie
1966   "Group work with older people in a settlement house." Pp. 91–96 in Louis Long and John Mogey (eds.), Theory and Practice in Social Work with the Aging. Boston: Boston University Council on Gerontology.
Allport, Gordon W.
1954   The Nature of Prejudice. New York: Doubleday.
Arluke, Arnold, Louanne Kennedy, and Ronald C. Kessler
1979   "Reexamining the sick role concept: an empirical assessment." Journal of Health and Social Behavior 20:30–36.
Arluke, Arnold, and John Peterson
1977   "Old age as illness: notes on accidental medicalization." A paper delivered at the Annual Meeting of the Society for Applied Anthropology, San Diego, California.
Arnhoff, F., and Irving Lorge
1960   "Stereotypes about aging and the aged." School and Society 88:70–71.
Aronoff, Craig
1974   "Old age in prime time." Journal of Communication 24:86–87.

Atchley, Robert C.
1975   "The life course, age grading, and age-linked demands for decision
            making." Pp. 261–278 in Nancy Datan and Leon H. Ginsberg
            (eds.), Lifespan Developmental Psychology: Normative Life
            Crises. New York: Academic Press.
1977   The Social Forces in Later Life. Second Edition. Belmont,
            California: Wadsworth.
Baltes, Paul B., and K. Warner Schaie
1974   "Aging and I.Q.—the myth of the twilight years." Psychology
            Today 7:35–38; 40.
Banks, James A.
1972   "Racial prejudice and the black self-concept."Pp. 5–36 in James
            A. Banks and Jean D. Grambs (eds.), Black Self-Concept. New
            York: McGraw-Hill.
Barron, Milton L.
1953   "Minority group characteristics of the aged in American society."
            Journal of Gerontology 8:477–482.
Barrow, G. M.
1971   "Physicians' attitude toward aging and the aging process." Ph.D.
            dissertation, Washington University.
Beasley, W. C.
1940   "The general problem of deafness in the population." Laryngo-
            scope 50:856–905.
de Beauvoir, Simone
1972   The Coming of Age. New York: G. P. Putnam's Sons.
Beeson, M. F.
1920   "Intelligence at senescence." Journal of Applied Psychology
            4:219–234.
Bell, B. D., and G. G. Stanfield
1973   "The aging stereotype in experimental perspective." Geron-
            tologist 13:341–344.
Bell, B., E. Wolf, and C. D. Bernholz
1972   "Depth perception as a function of age." Aging and Human De-
            velopment 3:77–81.
Bell, Tony
1967   "The relationship between social involvement and feeling old
            among residents in homes for the aged." Journal of Gerontology
            22:17–22.
Bellin, Seymour S.
1961   "Relations among kindred in later years of life: parents, their sib-
            lings and adult children." Paper read at American Sociological
            Association meeting, September 1, St. Louis, Missouri.
Bengtson, Vern L.
1969   "Differences between subsamples in level of present role ac-
            tivity." Pp. 35–49 in Robert J. Havighurst, J. M. Munnichs, B.
            Neugarten, and H. Thomas (eds.), Adjustment to Retirement: A
            Cross-National Study. New York: Humanities Press.
Bengtson, Vernon L., and Neal E. Cutler
1976   "Generations and intergenerational relations: perspectives on age
            groups and social change." Pp. 130–150 in Robert H. Binstock and
            Ethel Shanas (eds.), Handbook of Aging and the Social Sciences.
            New York: Van Nostrand Reinhold.

Bennet, Ruth G., and J. Eckman
1973 "Attitudes toward aging: a critical examination of recent literature and implications for future research." Pp. 575–597 in C. Eisdorfer and M. P. Lawton (eds.), The Psychology of Adult Development and Aging. Washington, D.C.: American Psychological Association.

Berger, M., and S. D. Rose
1977 "Interpersonal skill training with institutionalized elderly patients." Journal of Gerontology 32:346–353.

Bergman, M.
1971 "Hearing and aging: implications of recent research findings." Audiology 10:164–171.

Berry, Brewton, and Henry L. Tischler
1978 Race and Ethnic Relations. Boston: Houghton Mifflin.

Bettelheim, Bruno
1943 "Individual and mass behavior in extreme situations." Journal of Abnormal Psychology 38:424.

Binstock, R. H.
1972 "Interest-group liberalism and the politics of aging." Gerontologist 12:265–280.

Birren, James E.
1959 (ed.), Handbook of Aging and the Individual. Chicago: University of Chicago Press.
1968a "Aging: psychological aspects." Pp. 176–185 in David L. Sills (ed.), The International Encyclopedia of the Social Sciences. Volume 1. New York: Macmillan and the Free Press.
1968b "Psychological aspects of aging: intellectual functioning." Gerontologist 8:16–19.

Blau, Zena S.
1961 "Structural constraints on friendship in old age." American Sociological Review 26:429–439.
1973 Old Age in a Changing Society. New York: New Viewpoints.

Bock, E. Wilbur
1972 "Aging and suicide: the significance of marital, kinship, and alternative relations." Family Coordinator 21:71–80.

Bogomolets, A. A.
1946 The Prolongation of Life. New York: Duell, Sloan and Pearce.

Botwinick, Jack
1959 "Drives, expectancies, and emotions." Pp. 739–768 in James E. Birren (ed.), Handbook of Aging and the Individual. Chicago: University of Chicago Press.
1967 Cognitive Processes in Maturity and Old Age. New York: Springer.
1973 Aging and Behavior. New York: Springer.

Boucheron, Pierre
1959 How to Enjoy Life after Sixty. New York: Archer House.

Bowers, William H.
1952 "An appraisal of worker characteristics as related to age." Journal of Applied Psychology 33:296–300.

Braun, Harry W.
1959 "Perceptual processes." Pp. 543–561 in James E. Birren (ed.),

Handbook of Aging and the Individual. Chicago: University of Chicago Press.

Breen, Leonard Z.
1960   "The aging individual." Pp. 145–164 in Clark Tibbitts (ed.), Handbook of Social Gerontology. Chicago: University of Chicago Press.

Brink, William, and Louis Harris
1966   Black and White. New York: Simon and Schuster.

Bromley, D. B.
1974   The Psychology of Human Aging. Baltimore: Penguin Books.

Bunzel, J. H.
1972   "Note on the history of a concept—gerontophobia." Gerontologist 12:116–203.

Burg, A.
1967   "Light sensitivity as related to age and sex." Perceptual and Motor Skills 24:279–288.

Burgess, Ernest W.
1960   (ed.), Aging in Western Societies. Chicago: University of Chicago Press.

Butler, Robert N.
1969   "Age-ism: another form of bigotry." Gerontologist 9:243–246.
1974   "Successful aging and the role of the life review." Journal of American Geriatric Society 22:529–535.
1975   Why Survive? Being Old in America. New York: Harper and Row.

Butler, Robert N. and M. I. Lewis
1973   Aging and Mental Health. St. Louis, Missouri: C. V. Mosby.

Bynum, Jack E., B. L. Cooper, and Gene F. Acuff
1978   "Retirement reorientation: seminar adult education." Journal of Gerontology 33:253–261.

Cain, Leonard D.
1974   "The growing importance of legal age in determining the status of the elderly." Gerontologist 14:167–174.
1976   "Aging and the Law." Pp. 342–363 in Robert H. Binstock and Ethel Shanas (eds.), Handbook of Aging and the Social Sciences. New York: Van Nostrand Reinhold.

Carp, C. M.
1968   "Some components of disengagement." Journal of Gerontology 23:382–386.

Carp, Francis M.
1976   "Housing and living environments of older people." Pp. 248–264 in Robert H. Binstock and Ethel Shanas (eds.), Handbook of Aging and the Social Sciences. New York: Van Nostrand Reinhold.

Cavan, Ruth S.
1962   "Self and role in adjustment during old age." Pp. 526–536 in Arnold M. Rose (ed.), Human Behavior and Social Processes. Boston: Houghton-Mifflin.

Chatfield, W. F.
1977   "Economic and sociological factors influencing life satisfaction of the aged." Journal of Gerontology 32:593–599.

Ciliberto, David J.
1980   "The Influence of Perception of Old Age on Diagnosis." Unpublished master's thesis, Northeastern University, Boston.
Citrin, Richard S., and David N. Dixon
1977   "Reality orientation: a milieu therapy used in an institution for the aged." Gerontologist 17:39–43.
Clark, Kenneth B., and Mamie P. Clark
1958   "Racial identification and preference in Negro children." Pp. 602–611 in Eleanor E. Maccoby and others (eds.), Readings in Social Psychology. New York: Holt, Rinehart, and Winston.
Clark, M., and B. Anderson
1967   Culture and Aging. Springfield, Illinois: Charles C. Thomas.
Cole, Stephen, and Robert Lejeune
1972   "Illness and the legitimation of failure." American Sociological Review 37:347–356.
Comfort, Alex
1964a   Aging: The Biology of Senescence. New York: Holt, Rinehart and Winston.
1964b   The Process of Aging. New York: New American Library.
Cottrell, Fred
1955   Energy and Society. New York: McGraw-Hill.
1974   Aging and the Aged. Dubuque, Iowa: William C. Brown.
Cottrell, Fred, and Robert C. Atchley
1969   Women in Retirement: A Preliminary Report. Oxford, Ohio: Scripps Foundation.
Cowgill, Donald O.
1978   "Residential segregation by age in American metropolitan areas." Journal of Gerontology 33:446–453.
Cowgill, Donald O., and Lewelyn Holmes
1972   Aging and Modernization. New York: Appleton-Century-Crofts.
Craik, F. I. M.
1977   "Age differences in human memory." Pp. 384–420 in James Birren and K. W. Schaie (eds.), Handbook of the Psychology of Aging. New York: Van Nostrand Reinhold.
Cryns, A. G., and A. Monk
1972   "Attitudes of the aged toward the young: a multivariate study of intergenerational perception." Journal of Gerontology 27:107–112.
1973   "Attitudes toward youth as a function of adult age: a multivariate study of intergenerational dynamics." International Journal of Aging and Human Development 4:23–33.
Cumming, Elaine
1963   "Further thoughts on the theory of disengagement." International Social Science Journal 15:377–393.
Cumming, Elaine, and William E. Henry
1961   Growing Old: The Process of Disengagement. New York: Basic Books.
Cutler, Stephen
1973   "Perceived prestige loss and political attitudes among the aged." Gerontologist 13:69–75.

1974   "The effects of transportation and distance on voluntary associa-
            tion participation among the aged." International Journal of Aging
            and Human Development 5:81–94.
Davis, J. F.
1978   Minority-Dominant Relations. Arlington Heights, Illinois: AHM
            Publishing.
Davis, K.
1973   "Hospital cost and the medicare program." Social Security Bulle-
            tin 36(8):18–36.
Demerath, N. J., III, and R. A. Peterson
1967   System, Change and Conflict. New York: The Free Press.
Drevenstedt, Jean
1976   "Perceptions of onset of young adulthood, middle age, and old
            age." Journal of Gerontology 31:53–57.
Duvall, Evelyn
1971   Family Development. Fourth edition. Philadelphia: Lippincott.
Elkins, Stanley M.
1959   Slavery. Chicago: University of Chicago Press.
Epstein, L. A., and J. H. Murray
1968   "Employment and retirement." Pp. 354–356 in Bernice L.
            Neugarten (ed.), Middle age and aging. Chicago: University of
            Chicago Press.
Feifel, Herman
1957   "Judgement of time in younger and older persons." Journal of
            Gerontology 12:71–74.
Felstein, Ivor
1973   Sex in Later Life. Baltimore: Penguin Books.
Fischer, David Hackett
1977   Growing Old in America. New York: Oxford University Press.
Foster, J. C., and G. A. Taylor
1920   "The applicability of mental tests to persons over fifty years of
            age." Journal of Applied Psychology 4:39–58.
Francher, J. S.
1973   "It's the Pepsi generation . . . accelerated aging and the television
            commercial." International Journal of Aging and Human Devel-
            opment 4:245–255.
Frankfather, Dwight
1977   The Aged in the Community. New York: Praeger.
Frazier, E. Franklin
1949   The Negro in the United States. New York: Macmillan.
Freeman, Joseph T.
1960a   "The geriatric limb on the gerontology tree." Pp. 19–40 in Nathan
            W. Shock (ed.), Aging. New York: American Association for the
            Advancement of Science.
1960b   "The first fifty years of geriatrics (1909–1959)." Geriatrics
            15:216–217.
Friedenberg, Edgar Z.
1969   "The generation gap." Annals of the American Academy of Politi-
            cal and Social Science 382:32–42.
Furry, C. A., and Baltes, P. B.

1973   "The effect of age differences in ability-extraneous performance
            variables on the assessment of intelligence in children, adults, and
            the elderly." Journal of Gerontology 28:73–80.
Gans, Herbert J.
1972   "The positive functions of poverty." American Journal of Sociol-
            ogy. 2:275–289.
Garvin, Richard M., and Robert E. Burger
1968   Where They Go to Die: The Tragedy of America's Aged. New
            York: Delacorte Press.
George, L. K., and G. L., Maddox
1977   "Subjective adaptation to loss of the work role: a longitudinal
            study." Journal of Gerontology 32:456–462.
Gerbner, George, and Larry Gross
1976   "Living with television: the violence profile." Journal of Com-
            munication 26:172–199.
Glenn, Norval D.
1969   "Aging, disengagement, and opinionation." Public Opinion Quar-
            terly 33:17–33.
Glenn, Norval D., and Michael Grimes
1968   "Aging, voting, and political interest." American Sociological Re-
            view 33:563–575.
Glenn, Norval D., and Ted Hefner
1972   "Further evidence on aging and party identification." Public Opin-
            ion Quarterly 36:31–47.
Gold, Byron, Elizabeth Kutza, and Theodore R. Marmor
1976   "United States social policy on old age: present patterns and
            predictions." Pp. 9–22 in Bernice L. Neugarten and Robert J.
            Havighurst (eds.), Social Policy, Social Ethics, and the Aging So-
            ciety. Washington, D.C.: U.S. Government Printing Office.
Golde, P., and N. A. Kogan
1959   "A sentence completion procedure for assessing attitudes toward
            old people." Journal of Gerontology 14:355–363.
Goode, William J.
1964   The Family. Englewood Cliffs, New Jersey: Prentice-Hall.
Gouldner, Alvin W.
1970   The Coming Crisis of Western Sociology. New York: Basic Books.
Gray, Robert M., and Josephine M. Kasteler
1970   "An evaluation of the effectiveness of a foster grandparent proj-
            ect." Sociology and Social Research 54:181–189.
Greene, Mark R., and others
1969   Pre-retirement Counseling, Retirement, Adjustment and the Older
            Employee. Eugene, Oregon: University of Oregon Graduate
            School of Management.
Greenwald, Herbert J., and Don B. Oppenheim
1968   "Reported magnitude of self-misidentification among Negro
            children—an artifact?" Journal of Personality and Social Psychol-
            ogy 8:49–52.
Hall, G. Stanley
1923   Senescence: The Last Half of Life. New York: D. Appleton.

Hanaver, Joan
1976   "Senior set unhappy with TV's mirror." Patriot Ledger May 13,
          1976:12.
Harris, Louis, and Associates
1975   The Myth and Reality of Aging in America. New York: National
          Council on Aging.
Havighurst, Robert J.
1963   "Successful aging." Pp. 229–320 in Richard H. Williams, Clark
          Tibbitts and William Donahue (eds.), Processes of Aging. Volume
          1. New York: Atherton.
1968a   "Personality and patterns of aging." Gerontologist 8:20–23.
1968b   "A social-psychological perspective on aging." Gerontologist
          8:67–71.
Havighurst, Robert J., Bernice Neugarten, and S. Tobin
1964   "Disengagement, personality and life satisfaction." Pp. 319–324 in
          P. Hansen (ed.), Age with a Future. Copenhagen: Munksgaard.
Haynes, S. G., A. J. McMichael, and H. A. Tyroler
1977   "The relationship of normal involuntary retirement to early
          mortality among U.S. rubber workers." Social Science and
          Medicine 11:105–114.
Henry, W. E.
1964   "The theory of intrinsic disengagement." International Geron-
          tological Research Seminar, Markaryd, Sweden.
Heron, Alastair, and Shaila Chown
1967   Age and Function. Boston: Little Brown.
Hickey, Tom, Louise A. Hickey, and Richard A. Kalish
1968   "Children's perceptions of the elderly." Journal of Genetic
          Psychology 112:227–235.
Hinchcliffe, B.
1962   "Aging and sensory thresholds." Journal of Gerontology 17:45–
          50.
Hite, Shere
1976   The Hite Report. New York: Dell.
Hochschild, Arlie Russell
1973a   "Communal life styles for the old." Society 10 (No. 5):50–57.
1973b   The Unexpected Community. Englewood Cliffs, New Jersey:
          Prentice-Hall.
1975   "Disengagement theory: a critique and proposal." American
          Sociological Review 40(5):553–569.
Hovland, C. I.
1951   "Human learning and retention." Pp. 613–689 in S. S. Stevens
          (ed.), Handbook of Experimental Psychology. New York: John
          Wiley.
Howell, T. H.
1949a   "Old age." Geriatrics 4:281–292.
1949b   "Senile deterioration of the central nervous system." British Med-
          ical Journal 1(4592):56–58.
Hoyt, G. C.
1954   "The life of the retired in a trailer park." American Journal of
          Sociology 59:361–370.

Inkeles, A., and D. J. Levinson
1969   "National character: the study of modal personality and sociocultural systems." Pp. 418–506 in Gardner Lindzey and Elliot Aronson (eds.), Handbook of Social Psychology. Volume 4. Reading, Mass.: Addison Wesley.

Jacobs, Jerry
1974   Fun City: An Ethnographic Study of a Retirement Community. New York: Holt, Rinehart and Winston.

Jacobs, Ruth H., and Barbara H. Vinick
1977   Re-Engagement in Later Life. Stamford, Connecticut: Greylock.

Jarvik, Lissy
1979   Psychological Symptoms and Cognitive Loss in the Elderly. New York: Halsted.

Jerome, Edward A.
1959   "Age and learning-experimental studies." Pp. 655–699 in James E. Birren (ed.), Handbook of Aging and the Individual. Chicago: University of Chicago Press.

Jones, Harold E.
1959   "Intelligence and problem solving." Pp. 700–738 in James E. Birren (ed.), Handbook of Aging and the Individual. Chicago: University of Chicago Press.

Jones, Rochelle
1977   The Other Generation: The New Power of Older People. Englewood Cliffs, New Jersey: Prentice-Hall.

Kahana, Eva, Jersey Liang, Barbara Felton, Thomas Fairchild, and Zev Harel
1977   "Perspectives of aged on victimization, 'ageism,' and their problems in urban society." Gerontologist 17:121–129.

Kardiner, A.
1968   Letter to the editor of The Saturday Evening Post August 24, 1968:10.

Katz, Daniel, and Kenneth Braly
1933   "Racial stereotypes of one hundred college students." Journal of Abnormal and Social Psychology October-December, 280–290.

Kerckhoff, Alan C.
1964   "Husband-wife expectations and reactions to retirement." Journal of Gerontology 19:510–516.

King, H. F., and D. Speakman
1953   "Age and industrial accident rates." British Journal of Industrial Medicine 10:51–58.

Kinsey, Alfred C., W. B. Pomeroy, and C. R. Martin
1948   Sexual Behavior in the Human Male. Philadelphia: W. B. Saunders.

Kluckhohn, Florence R., and Fred L. Strodtbeck
1961   Variations in Value Orientations. New York: Harper and Row.

Kogan, Nathan
1961   "Attitudes toward old people: the development of a scale and an examination of correlates." Journal of Abnormal and Social Psychology 62:44–54.

Kohn, Robert B.
1971   Principles of Mammalian Aging. Englewood Cliffs, New Jersey: Prentice-Hall.

Koller, Marvin B.
1968   Social Gerontology. New York: Random House.
Konig, E.
1957   "Pitch discrimination and age." Acta oto-laryngologica 48:475–489.
Korenchevsky, V.
1950   "The problem of aging and the ways and means for achieving the rapid progress of gerontological research." Pp. 7–24 in New York Academy of Medicine, Social and Biological Challenge of Our Aging Population. New York: Columbia University Press.
Kornzweig, A. L., M. Feldstein, and J. Schneider
1957   "The eye in old age. IV. ocular survey of over one thousand aged persons with special reference to normal and disturbed visual function." American Journal of Ophthalmology 44:29–37.
Kreps, Juanita M.
1963   (ed.), Employment, Income, and Retirement Problems of the Aged. Durham, North Carolina: Duke University Press.
1966   Technology, Manpower and Retirement Policy. Cleveland, Ohio: World.
Kuhlen, Raymond G.
1968a   "Age and intelligence: the significance of cultural change in longitudinal versus cross-sectional findings." Pp. 552–562 in Bernice Neugarten (ed.), Middle Age and Aging. Chicago: University of Chicago Press.
1968b   "Developmental changes in motivation during the adult years." Pp. 115–136 in Bernice Neugarten (ed.), Middle Age and Aging. Chicago: University of Chicago Press.
Kuhn, Thomas S.
1962   The Structure of Scientific Revolutions. Chicago: University of Chicago Press.
Kumnick, Lillian S.
1956   "Aging and the latency and duration of pupil constriction in response to light and sound stimuli." Journal of Gerontology 11:391–396.
Lakowski, R.
1961   "Is the deterioration of color discrimination with age due to lens or retinal changes?" Pp. 69–86 in Tagungs-Bericht der Internationalen Farbtagung. Dusseldorf: Germany.
Landers, Ann
1977   Boston Globe, November 30:12.
Lawton, M. Powell
1974   "Social ecology and the health of older people." American Journal of Public Health 64:257–260.
Lehman, H.
1953   Age and Achievement. Princeton, New Jersey: Princeton University Press.
Lemon, B. W., K. L. Bengtson, and J. A. Peterson
1972   "An exploration of the activity theory of aging: activity types and life satisfaction among in-movers to a retirement community." Journal of Gerontology 27:511–523.

Lerner, Max
1957   America as a Civilization. Volume 2. New York: Simon and Schus-
            ter.
Levin, Jack
1975   The Functions of Prejudice. New York: Harper and Row.
Levin, Jack, and William C. Levin
1977   "Perceived age and willingness to interact with an old person." A
            paper presented at the Annual Meeting of the Eastern Sociological
            Society, New York.
Lewis, Oscar
1966   "The culture of poverty." Scientific American 16:19–25.
Lincoln, C. Eric
1961   The Black Muslims in America. Boston: Beacon Press.
Linn, L. S., and M. S. Davis
1972   "Physicians' orientation, drug use, and source of drug informa-
            tion." Social Science and Medicine 6:199–204.
Lippman, Walter
1922   Public Opinion. New York: Harcourt Brace Jovanovich.
Lipsitt, Don R.
1977   "Psychological barriers to getting well." Pp. 332–337 in Richard
            A. Kalish (ed.), The Later Years. Monterey, California: Brooks/
            Cole.
Lobsenz, Norman M.
1974   "Sex and the senior citizen." New York Times Magazine January
            20, 1974:8–34.
Long, Barbara H., Robert C. Ziller, and Elaine E. Thompson
1960   "A comparison of prejudices: the effects upon friendship ratings of
            chronic illness, old age, education, and race." Journal of Social
            Psychology 70:101–109.
Lynch, James J.
1977   The Broken Heart: The Medical Consequences of Loneliness in
            America. New York: Basic Books.
McFarland, Ross A., and Brian M. O'Doherty
1959   "Work and occupational skills." Pp. 452–502 in James E. Birren
            (ed.), Handbook of Aging and the Individual. Chicago: University
            of Chicago Press.
McKain, Walter
1972   "The aged in the U.S.S.R." Pp. 151–165 in D. O. Cowgill and L.
            D. Holmes (eds.), Aging and Modernization. New York:
            Appleton-Century-Crofts.
McTavish, Donald G.
1971   "Perceptions of old people: a review of research, methodologies,
            and findings." Gerontologist 11(4, part 2):90–101.
Maddox, George L., and James Wiley
1977   "Scope, concepts and methods in the study of aging." Pp. 3–34 in
            Robert Binstock and Ethel Shanas (eds.), Handbook of Aging and
            the Social Sciences. New York: Van Nostrand Reinhold.
Manaster, Al
1972   "Therapy with the 'senile' geriatric patient." International Journal
            of Group Psychotherapy 22:250–257.

Markson, Elizabeth W.
1971   "A hiding place to die." Transaction November/December, 1971:48–54.
Markson, Elizabeth W., Gary S. Levitz, and Maryvonne Gognalons-Caillard
1973   "The elderly and the community: reidentifying unmet needs." Journal of Gerontology 28:503–509.
Masters, William H., and Virginia Johnson
1966   Human Sexual Response. Boston: Little Brown.
Maves, Paul B.
1960   "Aging, religion, and the church." Pp. 698–742 in Clark Tibbitts (ed.), Handbook of Social Gerontology. Chicago: University of Chicago Press.
Mendelson, Mary Adelaide
1974   Tender Loving Greed. New York: Vintage Books.
Merton, Robert K.
1949   Social Theory and Social Structure. Glencoe, Illinois: The Free Press.
Miles, Catherine C.
1934   "The influence of speed and age on intelligence scores of adults." Journal of Genetic Psychology 10:208–210.
Miller, Stephen J.
1965   "The social dilemma of the aging leisure participant." Pp. 77–92 in Arnold M. Rose and Warren Peterson (eds.), Older People and their Social World. Philadelphia: F. A. Davis.
Mills, C. Wright
1943   "The professional ideology of social pathologists." American Journal of Sociology 49(2):165–180.
Mills, Jane
1972   "Attitudes of undergraduate students concerning geriatric patients." American Journal of Occupational Therapy 26:200–203.
Mindel, C. H., and C. E. Vaughan
1978   "A multidimensional approach to religiosity and disengagement." Journal of Gerontology 33:103–108.
Moberg, David O.
1965   "Religion in old age." Geriatrics 20:977–982.
Moberg, R. G.
1969   "Attitudes of ministers toward old people." Dissertation Abstracts 30:2619A.
Montagu, Ashley
1977   "Don't be adultish!" Psychology Today 11:46–50;55.
Morland, Kenneth J.
1972   "Racial acceptance and preference of nursery school children in a southern city." Pp. 51–58 in J. Brigham and T. Weissbach (eds.), Racial Attitudes in America. New York: Harper and Row.
Moynihan, Daniel P.
1965   The Negro Family: The Case for National Action. Washington, D.C.: U.S. Department of Labor, U.S. Government Printing Office.
Myrdal, Gunnar
1944   An American Dilemma: The Negro Problem and Modern Democracy. New York: Harper.

Neugarten, Bernice L.
1968   "Adult personality: toward a psychology of the life cycle." Pp.
            137–147 in Bernice Neugarten (ed.), Middle Age and Aging.
            Chicago: University of Chicago Press.
1970   "The old and young in modern societies." American Behavioral
            Scientist 14:13–24.
1977   "Personality and the aging process." Pp. 72–77 in Steven H. Zarit
            (ed.), Readings in Aging and Death: Contemporary Perspectives.
            New York: Harper and Row.
Neugarten, B. L., and Associates
1964   Personality in Middle and Late Life. New York: Atherton Press.
Newell, D. S.
1961   "Social structural evidence for disengagement." Pp. 37–74 in
            Elaine Cumming and William Henry (eds.), Growing Old. New
            York: Basic Books.
Newman, G., and C. R. Nichols
1960   "Sexual activities and attitudes in older persons." Journal of the
            American Medical Association 173:33–35.
Nisbet, Robert A.
1966   The Sociological Tradition. New York: Basic Books.
Offir, Carole
1974   "At 65, work becomes a four-letter word." Psychology Today
            March, 7:40.
Orbach, Harold L.
1961   "Aging and religion: a study of church attendance in the Detroit
            metropolitan area." Geriatrics 16:530–540.
Palmore, Erdman
1969   "Sociological aspects of aging." Pp. 33–69 in E. W. Busse and E.
            Pfeiffer (eds.), Behavior and Adaptation in Later Life. Boston:
            Little, Brown.
1970   "The effects of aging on activities and attitudes." Pp. 332–341 in
            E. Palmore (ed.), Normal Aging. Durham, North Carolina: Duke
            University Press.
1971   "Attitudes toward aging as shown by humor." Gerontologist
            11:181–186.
1972   "Compulsory versus flexible retirement: issues and facts." Geron-
            tologist 12:343–348.
1975   The Honorable Elders. Durham, North Carolina: Duke University
            Press.
Palmore, Erdman, and K. Manton
1974   "Modernization and status of the aged: international correla-
            tions." Journal of Gerontology 29:205–210.
*Palmore, Erdman, and F. Whittington
1971   "Trends in the relative status of the aged." Social Forces 50:
            84–91.
Parsons, Talcott
1959   "The social structure of the family." Pp. 241–274 in Ruth Anshen
            (ed.), The Family: Its Function and Destiny. New York: Harper
            and Row.
1960   "Toward a healthy maturity." Journal of Health and Human Be-
            havior 1:163–173.

1961   "An outline of the social system." In Talcott Parsons, Edward
            Shils, Kaspar Naegele and Jesse R. Pitts (eds.), Theories of Soci-
            ety. Glencoe, Illinois: The Free Press.
1963   "Old age as a consummatory phase." Gerontologist 3:35–43.
Parsons, Talcott, E. Shils, K. D. Naegele, and J. R. Pitts
1961   (eds.), Theories of Society. Glencoe, Illinois: The Free Press.
Parsons, Talcott, and N. J. Smelser
1959   Economy and Society. Glencoe, Illinois: The Free Press.
Payne, Raymond, Frank E. Gibson, and Barbara B. Pittard
1969   "Social influences in senile psychosis." Sociological Symposium
            Spring, 1:137–146.
Pedersen, Johannes T.
1976   "Age and change in public opinion." Public Opinion Quarterly
            Summer, 40:143–153.
Percy, Charles H.
1974   Growing Old in the Country of the Young. New York: McGraw-
            Hill.
Peters, G. R.
1971   "Self-conceptions of the aged, age identification, and aging."
            Gerontologist 11:69–73.
Peterson, D. A.
1972   "Financial adequacy in retirement: perceptions of older Ameri-
            cans." Gerontologist 12:379–383.
Pettigrew, Thomas F.
1964   A Profile of the Negro American. New York: Van Nostrand
            Reinhold.
1971   Racially Separate or Together. New York: McGraw-Hill.
Pfeiffer, Eric, Adrian Verwoerdt, and Hsioh-Shan Wang
1969   "Sexual behavior in aged men and women." Archives of General
            Psychiatry 19:756–758.
Phillips, Bernard S.
1957   "A role theory approach to adjustment in old age." American
            Sociological Review 22:212–217.
1961   "Role change, subjective age and adjustment: a correlational
            analysis." Journal of Gerontology 16:347–352.
Proshansky, H., and P. Newton
1968   "The nature and meaning of Negro self-identity." Pp. 104–114 in
            M. Deutsch and others (eds.), Social Class, Race, and Psycholog-
            ical Development. New York: Holt.
Raab, Earl
1973   Major Social Problems. New York: Harper and Row.
Reichard, Suzanne, Florine Livson, and Paul G. Petersen
1962   Aging and Personality. New York: John Wiley.
1968   "Adjustment to retirement." Pp. 178–180 in Bernice Neugarten
            (ed.), Middle Age and Aging. Chicago: University of Chicago
            Press.
Richman, J.
1977   "The foolishness and wisdom of age: attitudes toward the elderly
            as reflected in jokes." Gerontologist 17:210–219.
Riley, Matilda White

1971   "Social gerontology and the age stratification of society." Gerontologist 11(1, part 1):79–87.
1976   "Age strata in social systems." Pp. 189–217 in Robert H. Binstock and Ethel Shanas (eds.), Handbook of Aging and the Social Sciences. New York: Van Nostrand Rinehold.

Riley, Matilda W., and Anne Foner
1968   Aging and Society. Volume 1: An Inventory of Research Findings. New York: Russell Sage Foundation.

Riley, Matilda W., John W. Riley, Jr., and Marilyn E. Johnson
1969   Aging and Society. Volume 2: Aging and the Professions. New York: Russell Sage Foundation.

Roman, P., and P. Taietz
1967   "Organizational structure and disengagement: the emeritus professor." Gerontologist 7:147–152.

Rose, Arnold M.
1960   "The impact of aging on voluntary associations." Pp. 666–697 in Clark Tibbetts (ed.), Handbook of Social Gerontology. Chicago: University of Chicago Press.
1964   "A current issue in social gerontology." Gerontologist 4:45–50.
1965a   "Physical health and mental outlook among the aging." Pp. 210–269 in Arnold Rose and W. Peterson (eds.), Older People and Their Social World. Philadelphia: F. A. Davis.
1965b   "The subculture of aging: a framework for research in social gerontology." Pp. 201–209 in Arnold M. Rose and Warren A. Peterson (eds.), Older People and Their Social World. Philadelphia: F. A. Davis.

Rose, A. M., and W. A. Peterson
1965   Older People and their Social World. Philadelphia: F. A. Davis.

Rose, Charles L., and John M. Mogey
1972   "Aging and preference for later retirement." Aging and Human Development 3:45–62.

Rosen, Bernard, and Thomas H. Jerdee
1976   "The influence of age stereotypes on managerial decisions." Journal of Applied Psychology 61:428–432.

Rosenberg, George S.
1970   The Worker Grows Old. San Francisco: Jossey-Bass.

Rosenfeld, Albert
1976   Prolongevity. New York: Avon.

Rosow, Irving
1961   "Retirement housing and social integration." Gerontologist 1:85–91.
1962   "Old age: one moral dilemma of an affluent society." Gerontologist 2:182–195.
1974   Socialization to Old Age. Berkeley: University of California Press.

Rubin, Isadore
1965   Sexual Life After Sixty. New York: Basic Books.
1968   "The 'sexless older years'—a socially harmful stereotype." Annals of the American Academy of Political and Social Sciences 376:86–95.

Ryan, William
1971   Blaming the Victim. New York: Vintage.
Sagarin, Edward
1971   The Other Minorities. Waltham, Massachusetts: Ginn.
Schiffman, S.
1977   "Food recognition by the elderly." Journal of Gerontology
            32:586–592.
Schiffman, Susan, and Marcy Pasternak
1979   "Decreased discrimination of food odors in the elderly." Journal
            of Gerontology 34:73–79.
Schulz, J. H.
1976   The Economics of Aging. Belmont, California: Wadsworth.
Seefeldt, Carol, Richard K. Jantz, Alice Galper, and Kathy Serock
1977   "Using pictures to explore children's attitudes toward the el-
            derly." Gerontologist 17:506–512.
Seeman, Melvin
1956   "Intellectual perspective and adjustment to minority status." So-
            cial Problems January (3):142–153.
Settin, Joan M.
1978   "Comment: some thoughts about diseases presenting as senility."
            Gerontologist 18:71–72.
Shanas, Ethel
1962   The Health of Older People: A Social Survey. Cambridge, Massa-
            chusetts: Harvard University Press.
1968   "Family help patterns and social class in three countries." Pp.
            296–308 in Bernice Neugarten (ed.), Middle Age and Aging.
            Chicago: University of Chicago Press.
Shelton, A. J.
1965   "Igbo aging and eldership. Notes for gerontologists and others."
            Gerontologist 5:20–24.
Siegler, Ilene
1976   "Aging IQs." Human Behavior July (5):55.
Simpson, George E., and J. Milton Yinger
1972   Racial and Cultural Minorities. New York: Harper and Row.
Slater, Phillip E.
1963   "Cultural attitudes toward the aged." Geriatrics 18:308–314.
Smith, Mickey C.
1976   "Portrayal of the elderly in prescription drug advertising." Geron-
            tologist 16(4):329–334.
Srole, Leo
1956   "Social integration and certain corollaries: an exploratory study."
            American Sociological Review December (21):709–716.
Stannard, Charles L.
1973   "Old folks and dirty work: the social conditions for patient abuse
            in a nursing home." Social Problems Winter, 20(3):329–340.
Stieglitz, E. J. (ed.)
1954   Geriatric Medicine: Medical Care of Later Maturity. Philadelphia:
            J. B. Lippincott.
Strehler, Bernard L.
1962   Time, Cells, and Aging. New York: Academic Press.

Streib, Gordon F.
1965   "Are the aged a minority group?" Pp. 35–46 in Bernice Neugarten
            (ed.), Middle Age and Aging. Chicago: University of Chicago
            Press.
1976   "Social stratification and aging." Pp. 160–188 in Robert H.
            Binstock and Ethel Shanas (eds.), Handbook of Aging and the
            Social Sciences. New York: Van Nostrand Reinhold.
Streib, Gordon F., and Harold L. Orbach
1967   "Aging." Pp. 612–640 in P. E. Lazarsfeld and others (eds.), The
            Uses of Sociology. New York: Basic Books.
Streib, G. F., and C. J. Schneider
1971   Retirement in American Society. Ithaca, New York: Cornell Uni-
            versity Press.
Streib, Gordon F., and Wayne E. Thompson
1960   "The older person in a family context." Pp. 447–488 in Clark
            Tibbetts (ed.), Handbook of Social Gerontology. Chicago: Univer-
            sity of Chicago Press.
Sussman, Marvin B., and Lee Burchinal
1962   "Kin family network: unheralded structure in current conceptuali-
            zations of family functioning." Pp. 247–254 in Bernice L. Neugar-
            ten (ed.), Middle Age and Aging. Chicago: University of Chicago
            Press.
Taves, M. J., and G. D. Hansen
1963   "Seventeen hundred elderly citizens." Pp. 73–181 in Arnold M.
            Rose (ed.), Aging in Minnesota. Minneapolis: University of Min-
            nesota Press.
Thompson, W. E., G. F. Streib, and J. Kosa
1960   "The effect of retirement on personal adjustment: a panel
            analysis." Journal of Gerontology 15:165–169.
Thorpe, Earl E.
1971   "Chattel slavery and concentration camps." Pp. 56–72 in Ann J.
            Lane (ed.), The Debate over Slavery. Urbana: University of Il-
            linois Press.
Thune, J. M.
1967   "Racial attitudes of older adults." Gerontologist 7:179–182.
Townsend, Claire
1971   Old Age: The Last Segregation. The Center for Study of Respon-
            sive Law. New York: Grossman Publishers.
Treas, Judith
1977   "Family support systems for the aged: some social and demo-
            graphic considerations." Gerontologist 17:486–491.
Troll, Lillian E.
1971   "The family of later life: a decade review." Journal of Marriage
            and the Family 33:263–290.
Tuckman, Jacob, and Irving Lorge
1952a   "The attitudes of the aged toward the older worker for
            institutionalized and non-institutionalized adults." Journal of
            Gerontology 7:559–564.
1952b   "Attitudes toward old workers." Journal of Applied Psychology
            36:149–153.

1953a   "Attitudes toward old people." Journal of Social Psychology 37:249–260.
1953b   Retirement and the Industrial Worker: Prospect and Reality. New York: Columbia University Teachers College.
1954   "Classification of the self as young, middle-aged, or old." Geriatrics 9:534–36.
United States Department of Health, Education, and Welfare
1971   "Health in the later years of life." Washington, D.C.: U.S. Government Printing Office. Stock No. 17722–0178.
United States Senate Subcommittee on Housing for the Elderly
1962   "Housing for the elderly." Washington, D.C.: U.S. Government Printing Office.
Uzzell, O.
1953   "Institutional membership and class levels." Sociology and Social Research 37:390–394.
Verplanck, W. S.
1957   "A glossary of some terms used in the objective science of behavior." Psychology Review Part 2 (suppl.).
Vivrett, Walter K.
1960   "Housing and community settings for older people." Pp. 549–623 in Clark Tibbetts (ed.), Handbook of Social Gerontology. Chicago: University of Chicago Press.
Wake, S. B., and M. J. Sporakowski
1972   "An intergenerational comparison of attitudes towards supporting aged parents." Journal of Marriage and the Family 34:42–48.
Weale, R. A.
1963   The Aging Eye. New York: Harper and Row.
Weber, Max
1947   The Theory of Social and Economic Organization. Trans., A. M. Henderson and Talcott Parsons. Ed., Talcott Parsons. New York: Oxford University Press.
Wechsler, D.
1944   The Measurement of Adult Intelligence. Baltimore: Williams and Wilkins Co.
Weiss, Alfred D.
1959   "Sensory functions." Pp. 503–542 in James E. Birren (ed.), Handbook of Aging and the Individual. Chicago: University of Chicago Press.
Welford, Alan T.
1959   "Psychomotor performance." Pp. 562–613 in James E. Birren (ed.), Handbook of Aging and the Individual. Chicago: University of Chicago Press.
1977   "Motor performance." Pp. 450–496 in J. E. Birren and K. W. Schaie (eds.), Handbook of the Psychology of Aging. New York: Van Nostrand Reinhold.
Whipple, Charles
1977   As interviewed for "Now, the revolt of the old." Time October 10, 1977:26.

Wilhite, Mary J., and Dale M. Johnson
1976   "Changes in nursing students' stereotypic attitudes toward old people." Nursing Research 25:430–432.
Williams, R. H., and C. Wirths
1965   Lives Through the Years. New York: Atherton Press.
Willoughby, R. R.
1927   "Family similarities in mental-test abilities (with a note on the growth and decline of these abilities)." Genetic Psychology Monographs. 2:235–277.
Winiecke, Linda
1973   "The appeal of age segregated housing to the elderly poor." International Journal of Aging and Human Development 4:293–306.
Wirth, Louis
1945   "The problem of minority groups." Pp. 347–372 in Ralph Linton (ed.), The Science of Man in the World Crisis. New York: Columbia University Press.
Wood, V.
1971   "Age-appropriate behavior for older people." Gerontologist 11:74–78.
Zarit, S. H., and R. L. Kahn
1975   "Aging and adaption to illness." Journal of Gerontology 30:67–72.
Zelditch, M., Jr.
1964   "Cross-cultural analysis of family structure." Pp. 462–500 in Morris Christensen (ed.), Handbook of Marriage and the Family. Chicago: Rand McNally.
Zimberg, Sheldon
1974   "The elderly alcoholic." Gerontologist 14:221–224.
Zola, I. K.
1962   "Feeling about age among older people." Journal of Gerontology 17:65–68.

Index

Acceptance
  of prejudice and discrimination,
    98–101
  as resignation, 101–102
  and the retirement community, 102
  and social change, 117–118
Activity Theory, 44–55, 62, 64
Acuff, Gene F., 59
Adorno, T. W., 91
Aged
  blaming, 35–64
  characteristics of, 2–4
  consciousness raising of, 126–128
  expectations for, 97–98
  images of, 73–76
  and leisure ethic, 101
  as a minority group, 61, 65–96
  negative attitudes toward, 88
  reactions of, x
Age Discrimination in Employment Act,
  122
Ageism
  and avoidance, 103
  in Colonial America, 88
  cultural aspects of, 85–86, 95
  ego-defensive consequences of, 91
  and industrialization, 87, 93, 95–96
  and institutionalized care, 119–121
  and mass communication, 90–91
  and mass media, 119
  as a form of prejudice and
    discrimination, 72–73
  psychological sources of, 91–92
  reactions to, 97–114
  social sources of, 92–93
"Age rights," 110
Age stratification view, 63
Aggression, 110–113
Aging
  acceptance of, 98–102, 113, 115–116
  assumed cause of, 42
  assumed effect of, 42
  avoidance of, 102–109, 113–118
  as a biological phenomenon, 62
  chemical, 8–9
  and creativity, 15
  economic problems of, 26, 30
  physiological, 3, 4, 6–10, 33
  as a process, 2–3
  and sex, 15–16, 79–80, 100
  as a social problem, 1
  social theory of, 2
  sociological, 2, 19, 29

Aging (continued)
  theories of, 35–39
Albert, William C., 30
Albrecht, Ruth, 116
Alcohol and drug abuse, 108
Alessi, Edward, 120–121, 127
Allen, Fannie, 59
Allport, Gordon W., 61
Anderson, B., 47
Anticipatory socialization, 32
Arluke, Arnold, 107–108
Arnhoff, F., 85
Aronoff, Craig, 90
Atchley, Robert C., 13–14, 16, 26, 28,
  32, 46, 53, 94, 125
Attitudes of the elderly, 32–33
Avoidance
  and ageism, 103
  as destructive behavior, 106–109
  encouraging, 116–117
  of old age, 102–103
  and passing, 104–105
  and re-engagement, 104
  and the retirement community,
    105-106
  and social change, 117–118

Baltes, Paul B., 13–14, 81–82
Banks, James A., 99
Barron, Milton L., 66n
Barrow, G. M., 85
Baruch, Bernard, 102
Beasley, W. C., 11
deBeauvoir, Simone, 82–83, 93
Beeson, M. F., 13
Bell, B., 11
Bell, B. D., 103
Bellin, Seymour S., 21
Bengston, Vernon L., 26, 53, 69
Bennett, Ruth G., 85
Berger, M., 59–60
Bergman, M., 11
Bernholz, C. D., 11
Berry, Brewton, 68, 71
Bettelheim, Bruno, 106–107
Binstock, R. H., 111, 125
"Biological clock," 8, 33
Birren, James E., 10, 12–13, 82
Blaming the victim, ix, 36–38, 64
  and disengagement theory, 47–49
  and subculture theory, 56–57
Blau, Zena S., 21, 98

Bock, E. Wilbur, 109
Bogomolets, A. A., 8
Botwinick, Jack, 11, 13–14, 16
Boucheron, Pierre, 104–105
Bowers, William H., 80–81
Braly, Kenneth, 73
Braun, Harry W., 12
Breen, Leonard Z., 4, 18, 66n
Brink, William, 69
Bromley, D. B., 11, 15
Bunzel, J. H., 85, 94
Burchinal, Lee, 24, 31
Burg, A., 11
Burger, Robert E., 29, 30
Burgess, Ernest W., 32, 98
Butler, Robert, x, 73–74, 107, 108–109, 119–120
Bynum, Jack E., 59

Cain, Leonard D., 72
Carp, C. M., 46
Carp, Francis M., 71–72
Cavan, Ruth S., 109
Chown, Shaila, 5
Ciliberto, David J., 108
Citrin, Richard S., 59–60
Clark, Kenneth B., 47, 68
Clark, Mamie P., 47, 68
Comfort, Alex, 4, 5, 8
Consciousness raising, 126–128
Conservatism, 82–84
Cooper, B. L., 59
Cottrell, Fred, 9, 16, 25, 26, 28, 43, 46
Cowgill, Donald O., 29, 72, 87–88
Craik, F. I. M., 14
Cryns, A. G., 32–33, 110
"Culture of poverty," 36, 56
Cumming, Elaine, 21, 44–47, 48, 50, 51, 84
Cutler, Stephen, 28, 69, 85, 110

Dancey, Ric, 120–121
Davis, J. F., 65, 66n, 91
Davis, K., 30
Death, causes of, 6–7
Decline, ix, 30–31, 33
  in care, 24
  cosmetic, 6
  in creativity, 15
  and disengagement, 48, 84–85
  in employment status, 88–89

Decline (continued)
  intellectual, 81–82
  in learning performance, 13
  in liberty, 88
  mental, 82
  period of, 4
  physiological, 1, 6–10, 43–44
  psychological, 1, 10–19
  in role, 21–23
  in sensory and psychomotor
    processes, 3, 10–13, 42–43
  sexual, 79–80
  and subculture theory, 56
Dependence, 27
Disengagement Theory, 43–53, 61–64
  criticisms and refinements of, 46–47
  and decline, 48
  as a functionalist theory, 45, 49–53
  as a problem of the young, 62–64
  stereotypes of, 84–85
  and victim blaming, 47–49
Dixon, David N., 59–60
Drevenstedt, Jean, 102
Duvall, Evelyn, 23

Eckman, J., 85
Elkins, Stanley M., 67, 107
"Entire life cycle" criterion, 69–71
Exceptionalist programs, 38–39, 57–60, 64

Family relationships, 23–24
Feifel, Herman, 12
Felstein, Ivor, 11, 16
Fischer, David Hackett, 24, 86, 88
Foner, Anne, 24, 32, 33
Foster, J. C., 13
Franchez, J. S., 90
Frankfather, Dwight, 108
Frazier, E. Franklin, 67
Freeman, Joseph T., 1, 7, 8
Friedenberg, Edgar Z., 93
Fun City, 101, 104, 116
Functionalism, 49–53
Furry, C. A., 14

Gans, Herbert, 51
Garvin, Richard M., 29, 30
George, L. K., 46–47
Gerbner, George, 90

Geriatrics, 1
Gerontophobia, 93–95
Gibson, Frank E., 106, 107, 109
Glenn, Norval D., 83, 84–85
Gognalons-Caillard, Maryvonne, 120
Gold, Byron, 125, 126
Golde, P., 78
Goode, William J., 23
Gouldner, Alvin W., 41n
Gray, Robert M., 84
Gray Panthers, 68, 112, 122, 124–126
Greene, Mark R., 26
Greenwald, Herbert J., 68
Grimes, Michael, 84
Gross, Larry, 90

Hall, G. Stanley, 1
Hanaver, Joan, 90–91, 110
Hansen, G. D., 68, 102, 103
Harris, Louis, 33, 63, 68, 69
Harris Survey, 74–78
    on conservatism, 82
    on intelligence, 81
    on job performance, 80
    on old age avoidance, 102–103
Havighurst, Robert J., 19, 46–47, 84, 99
Health services, 29–31
Hefner, Ted, 83
Henry, W. E., 21, 44–47, 50, 51, 84
Heron, Alastair, 5
Hickey, Louise A., 86
Hickey, Tom, 86
Hinchcliffe, B., 11
Hite, Shere, 79–80
Hochschild, Arlie Russess, 29, 46, 105–106
Holmes, Lewelyn, 72, 87–88
House Select Committee on Aging, 112
Hovland, C. I., 13
Howell, T. H., 8, 11
Hoyt, G. C., 29

Inkeles, A., 17–18
Institutional care, 119–121
Intelligence and I.Q., 13–14, 81–82
"Interpersonal skill training," 59
Isolation, 3

Jacobs, Jerry, 101, 102, 103, 105, 116
Jacobs, Ruth, 46, 63, 104
Japanese elders, 89–90

Jarvik, Lissy, 82
Jerdee, Thomas H., 63, 76–77
Jerome, Edward A., 13
Johnson, Dale M., 85
Johnson, Virginia, 15–16, 79
Jokes and quotations, 76
Jones, Harold E., 14
Jones, Rochelle, 118

Kahana, Eva, 103
Kahn, R. L., 107
Kalish, Richard A., 86
Kardiner, A., 41
Kasteler, Josephine M., 84
Katz, Daniel, 73
Kennedy, Louanne, 108
Kessler, Ronald C., 108
King, H. F., 12
Kinsey, Alfred C., 79
Kluckhohn, Florence R., 94, 97
Kogan, Nathan, 78, 92
Kohn, Robert, 8–9
Koller, Marvin B., 14, 23–24
Konig, E., 11
Korenchevsky, V., 8
Kornsweig, A. L., 11
Kosa, J., 26
Kreps, Juanita M., 27
Kuhlen, Raymond G., 13, 17
Kuhn, Thomas S., ix
Kumnick, Lillian S., 11
Kutza, Elizabeth, 125, 126

Lakowski, R., 11
Lehman, H., 15
Lemon, B. W., 53
Lerner, Max, 121
Levin, Jack, 72, 73, 77–78, 91
Levin, William C., 77–78
Levinson, D. J., 17–18
Levitz, Gary S., 120
Lewis, Oscar, 36, 56, 107, 108, 109
L.I.F.E., 120–121
Lincoln, C. Eric, 67, 98–99
Linn, L. S., 91
Lippman, Walter, 73
Lipsett, Don R., 108
Livson, Florine, 18
Lobsenz, Norman M., 15–16, 100
Long, Barbara H., 78
Lorge, Irving, 63, 74, 76, 84, 85, 102, 105
Lynch, James J., 30

McFarland, Ross A., 12
McKain, Walter, 90, 100
McTavish, Donald G., 22, 32, 74
Maddox, George L., 40, 46
Manaster, Al, 117
Manton, K., 88–89
Markson, Elizabeth W., 120–121
Marmor, Theodore R., 125, 126
Martin, C. R., 79
Masters, William H., 15–16, 79
Maves, Paul B., 28
Medicare, 30, 118
Medicine, geriatric, 7
Memory, 14
Mendelson, Mary Adelaide, 29, 30
Merton, Robert K., 51
Miles, Catherine C., 13
Miller, Stephen J., 101
Mills, C. Wright, 40–41
Mills, Jane, 85
Mindel, C. H., 46
Minority group concept, 10, 61, 65–96
Moberg, David O., 28
Moberg, R. G., 85
Mogey, John M., 85
Monk, A., 32–33, 110
Montagu, Ashley, 100
Morland, Kenneth G., 68
Motivation, 16–17
Moynihan, Daniel P., 36

National Council on Aging, 74, 80
Negative group consciousness, 67–68
Neugarten, Bernice L., 18–19, 22,
    110–111
Newell, D. S., 46
Newman, G., 79
Newton, P., 99
Nichols, C. R., 79
Nisbet, Robert A., 41
Norms, 31–33
Nursing home care, 30, 58

O'Doherty, Brian M., 12
Offir, Carole, 112
Old age
    characteristics of, 75–76
    criteria of, 71–72
    denial of, 102
Oppenheim, Don B., 68
Orbach, Harold H., 2, 28

Palmore, Erdman, 26, 66n, 76, 83–84,
    88–89, 94
Parsons, Talcott, 24, 49–50, 108, 120
Passing, 104–105
Pasternak, Marcy, 11, 16
Payne, Raymond, 106, 107, 109
Pederson, Johannes T., 83
Perceptual processes, 11–12
Percy, Charles H., 103, 112–113
Personality, 17–19
Peters, G. R., 103
Peterson, D. A., 110
Peterson, J. A., 53
Peterson, John, 107–108
Peterson, Paul G., 18, 25
Pettigrew, Thomas F., 68, 97
Pfeiffer, Eric, 79
Phillips, Bernard S., 21, 22, 45n, 103
Pittard, Barbara B., 106, 107, 109
Pomeroy, W. B., 79
Prejudice, 72–73
Problem solving, 14
Proshansky, H., 99
Psychological deterioration, 1, 42–43

Raab, Earl, 40
Reality orientation, 59–60
Re-engagement, 104, 106
Reichard, Suzanne, 18, 25
Religion, 28
Retirement, 25, 26, 59
    as a form of age discrimination, 121
    forced, elimination of, 122–124
    mandatory, 93, 109, 122
    reducing pressures toward, 122
Retirement community, 102
    and avoidance, 105–106
    Fun City, 101, 104, 116
    Merrill Court, 105, 106
Richman, J., 76
Riley, Matilda White, 24, 32, 33, 54, 63,
    99, 109
"Role exits," 98
Role loss, 21–23, 30–31, 46–47
    adjustment to, 3
    and change, 21–22
    measuring, 21
    and societal disengagement, 24
Roman, P., 46
Rose, Arnold M., 28, 44, 46, 54, 56, 59,
    66n, 101–102, 110
Rose, Charles L., 85

Rosen, Bernard, 63, 76–77
Rosenberg, George S., 26
Rosenfeld, Albert, 94
Rosow, Irving, 29, 32, 54–56, 63, 66n, 94–95, 98, 109
Rubin, Isadore, 16, 79, 80, 100
Russian elders, 90
Ryan, William, 36, 43, 48, 56, 57, 60–61, 62–63

Sagarin, Edward, 65
"Savage discovery," 43
Schaie, Warner, 13–14, 81–82
Schiffman, Susan, 11, 16
Schneider, J., 11, 25, 26
Schulz, J. H., 27, 72, 73
Seefeldt, Carol, 86
Seeman, Melvin, 68
Self-fulfilling prophecy, 100–101
Senate Special Committee on Aging, 111
Senescence, 1, 4–5
Senility, 106–108
Senior citizen
    avoidance of, 106
    role of, 97–98, 99–101, 110, 114, 118
Sensory threshold, 10–12
    loss of, 6, 42–43
Service Corps of Retired Executives and Active Corps of Executives, 117
Services, community-based, 28–29
Settin, Joan M., 106
Shanas, Ethel, 24, 29
Shelton, A. J., 107
Siegler, Ilene, 82
Simpson, George E., 68, 92, 108
Slater, Phillip E., 125
Smelser, N. J., 50
Social gerontology, x, 2
Socialization, 20–21
Social order, 39–41
Social Security, 71, 122, 123
Societal disengagement, 24
Speakman, D., 12
Sporakowski, M. J., 85
Srole, Leo, 92
Stannard, Charles L., 119
Stereotypes, 73, 76–85
    of conservatism, 82–84
    and discrimination, 76–78
    of disengagement, 84–85
    of intelligence, 81–82
    of job performance, 76–78
    of sexual inactivity, 79

Stieglitz, E. S., 1–2
Strehler, Bernard, 4–5, 8
Streib, Gordon F., 2, 23, 24, 25, 26, 42, 46, 66
Strodtbeck, Fred L., 94, 97
Subculture theory, 54–57, 62, 64
Suicide, 109
Sussman, Marvin, B., 24, 31
System changes, 124–128

Taietz, P., 46
Taves, M. J., 68, 102, 103
Taylor, G. A., 13
Thompson, Elaine E., 23, 24, 26, 78
Thorpe, Earl E., 99
Thune, J. M., 32
Tischler, Henry, 68, 71
Tobin, S., 18–19
Townsend, Claire, 29
Treas, Judith, 24
Troll, Lillian E., 24
Tuckman, Jacob, 63, 74, 76, 84, 85, 102, 105

United States Department of Health, Education and Welfare, 6, 11, 29
United States Social Security Administration, 119
United States Subcommittee on Housing for the Elderly, 29
Universalist program, 39, 57–60, 64
Uzzell, O., 28

"Variant value orientation," 97
Vaughan, C. E., 46
Verplanck, W. S., 11
Verwoerdt, Adrian, 79
Vinick, Barbara H., 103, 104
Vivrett, Walter K., 29
Voluntary associations, 28
Volunteer work, 58–59, 116, 118

Wake, S. B., 85
Wang, Hsioh-Shan, 79
Weale, R. A., 11
Weber, Max, 66–67
Wechsler, D., 13
Welford, Alan T., 12
Whipple, Charles, 123
White House Conference on Aging, 124
Whittington, F., 66n

Wiley, James, 40
Wilhite, Mary J., 85
Williams, R. H., 47
Willoughby, R. R., 13
Winiecke, Linda, 29
Wirth, Louis, 65
Wirths, C., 47
Wolf, E., 11
Wood, V., 98

Yinger, J. Milton, 68, 92, 108
"Youth culture," 31

Zarit, S. H., 30, 107
Zelditch, M. Jr., 23
Ziller, Robert C., 78
Zimberg, Sheldon, 108
Zola, I. K., 102